D1276158

VITAMINS FOR YOUR **SOUL**

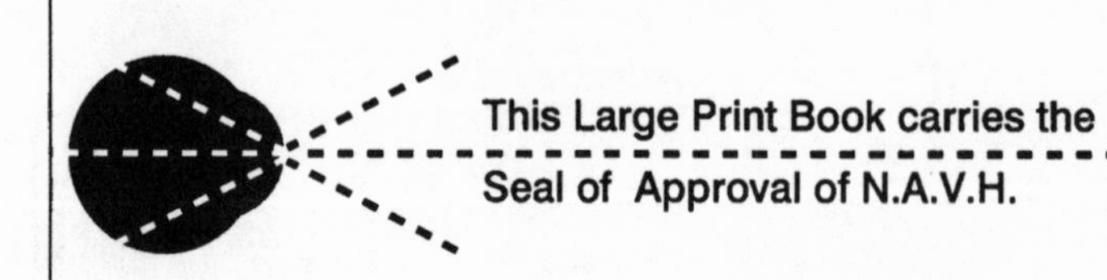
This Large Print Book carries the
Seal of Approval of N.A.V.H.

VITAMINS FOR YOUR SOUL

200 Ways to Nurture Your Spiritual Life

TRACI MULLINS
& ANN SPANGLER

**G.K. Hall & Co.
Thorndike, Maine**

Published in 1998 by arrangement with Doubleday,
a division of Bantam Doubleday Dell Publishing Group, Inc.

G.K. Hall Large Print Inspirational Collection.

The text of this Large Print edition is unabridged.
Other aspects of the book may vary from the original edition.

Set in 16 pt. Plantin by Al Chase.

Printed in the United States on permanent paper.

Library of Congress Cataloging in Publication Data

Mullins, Traci, 1960–
Vitamins for your soul: 200 ways to nurture your spiritual life / Traci Mullins & Ann Spangler.
p. cm.
Includes bibliographical references.
ISBN 0-7838-8330-7 (lg. print : hc : alk. paper)
1. Spiritual life. 2. Soul. I. Spangler, Ann. II. Title.
[BL624.M8535 1998]
291.4′4—dc21 97-41488

To Judy, Susan, and Liz —
my soulmates for life.
(TM)

To Jack —
you got me started on the journey.
(AS)

Soul making has something to do with paying attention to the Things Invisible, things which do not lend themselves to manipulation and control. Things which contribute to the making of a soul will not succumb to being treated as problems to be solved. Soul making requires a move away from the need and desire to control to a waiting on the mystery at the heart of things.[1]

— ALAN JONES

[1] As quoted in Phil Cousineau, ed., *Soul, an Archaeology*, p. 142.

CONTENTS

• INTRODUCTION •

SOUL HUNGER

Man does not **have** *a soul;*
he **is** *one.*[1]
— HAROLD BRUCE HUNTING

We humans have a lot to cope with. The demands on us are ceaseless, the opportunities endless. We spend a great deal of our lives working, another share sleeping. In between we try to spend quality time with family and friends, pursue hobbies, exercise, keep our homes maintained, and enjoy whatever entertainment suits our style. In the crush of activity, we often forget to nurture one of the most important parts of ourselves.

And so it cries out. It growls with hunger. Because it's not made to be ignored.

Just as our bodies need sustenance, rest, exercise, and protection in order to thrive, our souls need refreshment and refueling, retreat and activity, attention and healing. Webster's describes the soul as the "vital or essential part." It contains the unique essence of who we are, the capacity we have to experience meaning in life and in relationship with ourselves, others, and God. It provides the essential connectors to the world around us and to the one within us. Ultimately, the soul is our bridge to God. Unless we cultivate a healthy soul, we starve emotionally, relationally, and spiritually.

Fortunately, it's not as hard to nurture and strengthen your soul as you might think. You might have to review your priorities and adjust your schedule a bit, but tending to your soul can be a natural, enjoyable part of your daily lifestyle.

The ideas throughout this book are intended to remind you that your soul not only exists, but it is hungry and lively and essential to your ability to engage in a world that needs you to be spiritually awake. By paying attention to your soul's needs and using some of these ideas to nurture your spiritual life, you will find that with regular practice the rewards can be life-changing. You will begin to experience the refreshment your soul craves and the serenity that comes from being deeply and meaningfully connected to the world and to God. You will find new energy to engage with other human beings who long for soul-to-soul interaction.

Each chapter in this book offers twenty ways for you to actively nourish your soul and enrich the souls of others. Because your soul needs different things at different times in your life, allow yourself to use only what you need on a given day. You may want to skim through the entire book to get yourself thinking in "soul language" and tune in to parts of yourself you've been neglecting. Once you're aware of what the book has to offer, you'll know where to turn for ideas and inspiration for particular needs or challenges.

You don't have to do everything this book suggests in a month, a year, or even a lifetime. Some days just reading a few of the quotes throughout each chapter will give you fresh perspective, or doing one simple activity will jump-start your sluggish spirit. A soul that is fed and cared for is a soul awake, alert, engaged, purposeful, and vibrant. A soul that lives produces a person who loves, and isn't that what it's all about in the end?

By offering suggestions for invigorating your spiritual life, we hope to encourage you to take small steps toward opening your soul to greater realities. This little book merely skims the surface of all that could be said about nurturing the life of the soul. Our purpose is to offer an appetizer, to whet your spiritual appetite for more.

If you're hungry, tired, curious, or just

plain excited about the potential of your soul, use this book often. Let it be a companion on your spiritual journey. Practice taking care of a part of yourself that you too often ignore. You will be glad you did. And so will the people in your world.

— Traci Mullins
— Ann Spangler
January 20, 1997

•1•

THE CARE & FEEDING OF YOUR SOUL

The man who has no inner life is the slave of his surroundings.[1]

— Henri Frederic Amiel

Think about your typical day. Perhaps it's up at 6 A.M., a quick cup of coffee and half a bagel while you help get the kids fed and read the headlines. You scream out of the driveway at 7:15 in order to make the first conference call at 8, then it's the usual day at the office: mountains of paperwork, meetings of questionable value, and those constant interruptions. Your two evening hours are packed with an attempt at "quality time" with the family and maybe half a chapter of that novel you've been pacing through for three months. Hardly a spare minute to think about something as invisible and unproductive as your soul, right?

Perhaps your day starts off a little more quietly. You don't have to get up until 7:30, you read the whole newspaper, and actually make oatmeal with old-fashioned oats. But the demands of the day still catch up to you:

kids and friends and phone calls and chores and that project you promised to finish by 6 P.M.

Let's face it: Life is *busy*. And even when it isn't, we fritter away time and wonder where it went. With all there is to do and enjoy, the needs of our souls are easy to overlook.

Before you can feed and care for your soul effectively, you must know what it needs. You must learn to listen to it and recognize its cries for attention. If you've let the demands of life drown out your soul's voice, you will have to put some effort into rediscovering that essential part of yourself. But your soul will always let you know what it wants — if you'll listen.

The fact that you're reading this book means that you're ready to pay more attention to your soul. What has drawn you to do this? Perhaps, in theologian Richard Foster's words, "somewhere in the subterranean chambers of your life you have heard the call to deeper, fuller living. Perhaps you have become weary of frothy experiences and shallow teaching. Every now and then you have caught glimpses, hints of something more than you have known. Inwardly you have longed to launch out into the deep."[2]

Spend some time thinking through your motivations for nurturing your spiritual life. When you know *why* you're doing something, you may be more successful in sticking with it. If the benefits of nourishing your soul are clear and compelling, you'll stay committed to your journey even when life's daily demands vie for your attention.

Before you begin nourishing your spiritual life with the "vitamins" this book offers, spend a few minutes writing down your reasons for caring for and feeding your soul. Nurturing your spiritual life is not all work and no play, as this book will show you. But shaping a healthy soul requires a steady diet of carefully chosen spiritual nutrients. It may take you a while to find out what your unique nutritional needs are, but once you do, you will never feel the same. You'll want to keep coming back for more.

> *What good would it do to get everything you want and lose you, the real you?*[3]
>
> — Jesus Christ

•1• As an outward expression of your desire to care for your soul, set aside at least thirty minutes this week to sit quietly and listen.

Ask yourself what you need to feel nourished and whole. Write down what you hear and refer to it periodically in the months ahead.

•2• Nutritionists tell us that breakfast is the most important meal of the day. Why not start your days with "breakfast for the soul" — fifteen minutes during which you thank God for his blessings, read inspirational books, listen for guidance, ask for help.

•3• Take a thirty-minute walk by yourself with the sole agenda of tuning into your inner world. Use the time to find out what's going on inside, to come up with a solution to a problem, to pray, or just to be.

> *Longing and desire play a great part in soul making. It is as if God has deliberately put unfulfilled desires into our hearts so that our hearts may be stretched beyond their present capacity. Soul making requires this kind of stretching. It is not enough to know about soul making, although there are some who like to dabble in a kind of psychic horticulture. Such dabbling is merely a device to avoid the genuine birth of the soul. It is an invidious form of resistance to the very life for which the soul longs.*[4]
>
> — ALAN JONES

•4• Any good graphic designer knows that cramming too much type on a page makes for unreadable text. "White space," space without anything on it, makes the page easier to read and more pleasing to the eye. Have you designed any "white space" into the pages of your own life — times to relax and drink in the moment? If not, eliminate two things from your schedule that you don't really need to do today. Resist the temptation to replace them with something else.

•5• List five ways you think the health of your soul affects the people in your world. Share your insights with a trusted friend and ask him or her to help keep you accountable for caring for your soul every day.

•6• Think about people you know, famous or not, living or dead, who seem to be people with rich souls. What qualities do you see in them that you would like to nourish in your own life? List them.

> *Think of yourself as a seed patiently wintering in the earth; waiting to come up a flower in the Gardener's good time, up into the real world, the real waking.*[5]
>
> — C. S. Lewis

•7• If you could change one thing about yourself, what would it be? (Hair color, height, and body shape are off limits in this exercise.) Chances are you've tried and failed. Surrender it, no matter how small or large. Tell God that your weakness is his opportunity. Humbly ask him to change what needs to be changed. Then watch for his power to be made perfect in your weakness.

•8• Think about something you've always wanted to do: take piano lessons, go surfing in Oahu, have lunch with a monk, ride in a hot-air balloon, pan for gold, visit the Holy Land; and promise yourself you'll find a way to do it in the next year.

•9• Go to bed early one night and get up in time to see the sunrise. Brew an especially good cup of coffee, tea, or cocoa and settle in for some quiet "soul time." Watch the world change color and listen to the sounds of everybody waking — the wild creatures outside and the "little critters" down the hall.

•10• Think about some of the frustrating experiences you've had in the past two weeks. Perhaps something or someone is trying to get your attention. What might the message be?

I can find nothing with which to compare the great beauty of a soul and its great capacity. The very fact that His Majesty says it is made in His image means that we can hardly form any conception of the soul's great dignity and beauty.[6]

— ST. TERESA OF ÁVILA

•11• Remember how much fun you had as a kid, armed only with crayons and drawing paper? You made pictures of familiar things: your house, your family, a tree, green grass and bright sun in a blue sky. Get out a box of crayons and some paper and draw a simple picture of your soul. What color is it right now? What shape? What does your drawing tell you about where you are on your spiritual journey?

•12• What does it look like on a daily basis for you to be "spiritually awake"? Write down your thoughts and keep them in a place where you'll be reminded of this ideal. Do you agree with the statement that the world needs you to be spiritually awake?

•13• Practicing gratitude is a habit that will increase your joy and the richness of your soul. Begin each day this week by writing down one thing for which you are grateful.

Then take short breaks throughout your day to say a silent prayer of thanksgiving.

> *There is no shortage of good days. It is good lives that are hard to come by. A life of good days lived in the senses is not enough. The life of sensation is the life of greed; it requires more and more. The life of the spirit requires less and less; time is ample and its passage sweet.*[7]
>
> — ANNIE DILLARD

•14• Draw the face of a clock on a piece of paper. What time is it in your life? Fill in the clock's hands with the first answer that comes to you. Then write a few lines about what this time means to you.

•15• Make a "God Box" — a shoebox with a slit in the lid will do. Each day write down something you're worrying about and put it in your God Box. Throughout the day, when the worry returns, remind yourself you have given it to God to take care of.

•16• Finish this sentence in as many ways as you can: "If my soul was well cared for, I would . . ." What benefits can you look forward to as you pay closer attention to your soul?

•17• If you don't schedule time to be alone and listen to God, you probably won't do it. Block off a half hour of time on your calendar this week and make your "appointment with God" the most important engagement on your schedule.

> *We are not simply hungry, we are famished. We have no idea how to satisfy the craving of our souls. Something happened in the rebellion that left us crazed with desire. We lost our bread, and we don't know how to get it back. In fact, we're not even sure what it looks like. If we could rediscover this bread, we could discontinue our meaningless pursuits. We could settle down for the feast that is not a lie. We could know, at last, contentment.*[8]
>
> — CHARLES TURNER AND GREGORY POST

•18• Think of a time when you experienced a spiritual awakening of some kind. Describe it to someone who cares about you, and tell him or her what it means to you today.

•19• Spend some time meditating on this statement: "I would rather live in a world where my life is surrounded by mystery than live in a world so small that my mind could comprehend it."[9] Then acknowledge to yourself and to God that you are not wise enough to know exactly what your soul needs from moment to moment. Commit yourself to regularly asking what God wants to teach you.

•**20**• "And the LORD God formed man of the dust of the ground, and breathed into his nostrils the breath of life; and man became a living soul."[10] What does this quote from the Book of Genesis in the Hebrew Scriptures say to you about your soul?

> *Life is so full of meaning and purpose, so full of beauty beneath its covering, that you will find earth but cloaks your heaven. Courage, then, to claim it, that is all! But courage you have, and the knowledge that we are pilgrims wending through unknown country on our way home.*[11]
>
> — Fra Angelico

•2•

A TOUCH OF WONDER

Hunting God is a great adventure.[1]
— Marie De Floris

Remember what it was like to be four years old? Probably not. Maybe this scene will refresh your memory. . . .

A little child and a caterpillar. Suddenly he sees it scooting along the sidewalk — bunching, wiggling as the caterpillar makes its way toward a leafy lunch. Wide-eyed, he reaches out to touch its furry spine and jerks his finger back, giggling. Again he reaches out, and this time he's rewarded with a prickly curl around his index finger, tiny sucking sensations from the creature's sixteen legs. He laughs out loud, staring intently at a part of God's creation he never imagined existed. His whole being is captivated, drenched in a moment of wonder and delight.

Is that feeling of being four years old coming back to you now? Everything was amazing! When you learned that a bulky, awkward little caterpillar transformed itself into a bright yellow butterfly, you couldn't take it in! The smallest things captivated your attention and blew your young brain circuits again and again. No matter what daily life was like for you, you could be swept away in a wondrous moment. In your little way, you touched God.

And then life happened. As you got older, you probably stepped on a few of the caterpillars you once stopped the world to gaze upon. The miracle of a butterfly became ho-hum, and you lost something essential. You lost touch with part of your soul.

If you want to wake up a part of your self that may have been sleeping for many years, open your eyes and heart to wondrous moments. Let them touch you. Rediscover what makes your eyes open wide and your child-heart giggle and gasp. Pay attention to the ordinary miracles of every day, to the awesome creation all around you. Look for a caterpillar. Reflect on the mind-boggling realities of deep space. Notice the transparent fingernails of a newborn child. Throw back your head and let the snowflakes swirl into your eyes.

Sometimes all our souls need to stir and dance is a touch of wonder . . . an attentive or playful moment . . . a startling experience of beauty. Let the four-year-old in you guide you to that moment today.

> *There is, and will forever be, a link between the innocence of childhood and the soul of the land. Our innocence allows us to perceive the magic of creation. We remain under its spell until the onset of adulthood; then the bond is broken, the intimacy lost, as we surrender to a world of our own making, where everything is quantified and known.*[2]
>
> — Valerie Andrews

•1• Make a trip to your local zoo. Take your time at each exhibit, reading all the informational plaques about each animal. You'll be amazed at the infinite diversity and creativity reflected in what you see.

•2• Check out a book from the library about the life and behaviors of any insect you can think of. Reflect on the artistry and perfection that created a gigantic and intricate buzzing, crawling, flying, stinging, mating world that you may rarely think about or appreciate.

•3• Next time you read a newspaper or newsmagazine, look for articles about the latest space research and discoveries. Let your mind reel.

Did you know that after thousands of years of research, astronomers have only begun to discover the facts about the universe? In 1996, the Hubble Space Telescope photographed the faintest galaxies ever observed, increasing the estimated number of galaxies in the universe from 10 billion to 50 billion. The galaxies photographed are some 4 billion times dimmer than what is visible to the naked eye. Seen from the earth, the telescope's target was about the size of a large grain of sand held at arm's length. Our galaxy, the Milky Way, is just one of the billions of galaxies in the universe, and in the Milky Way alone we have approximately 2 billion stars, and each star may have planets around it. Stars like the sun live 10 billion years and then burst into red giants 50 times their original size. As the stars explode, they create basic elements that are recycled into new stars, planets, and even life.

•4• Spend an evening stargazing. Take time to meditate on the power and workmanship of a Creator who formed both you and the constellations . . . and galaxy upon galaxy.

•5• Start making a list of simple things and experiences that give you joy and refresh your soul. It could be anything: the cool, ethereal glow of a sunrise; digging your toes in warm sand; a moist forest trail; the smell of freshly mowed grass; a child's bubbling laughter; a puppy's wet kisses; the woodwind call of a pigeon. Keep your list and add to it. Make a point of including at least one thing on your list in your experience of life every week.

•6• Next time you pass a variety of flowers in a yard or garden, *stop.* Spend a few minutes breathing in the unique aroma of each bloom. Allow yourself a simple pleasure.

> *The wind, one brilliant day, called to my soul with an aroma of jasmine.*[3]
>
> — ANTONIO MACHADO

•7• Attend a community festival that draws lots of young children and pay close attention to the kids around you who play, laugh, wonder, and fully participate in their surroundings. Better yet, take a child with you and let her remind you how to invite a touch of wonder into your day.

•8• Walk barefoot on a spongy, lush summer lawn.

•9• Find a spot in nature that is as free of human traffic as possible. Sit down and close your eyes for at least ten minutes, listening for every sound around you. Notice that even the quietest place in nature is alive with the activity of creation, and each sound has its own quality.

> *What is unique about a moment that has the power to bless us and the potential to feed us is not so much the power of the moment itself, but rather the quality of presence we bring to that moment. Our presence can change an ordinary, unnoticed moment into a moment of beauty that can feed the soul. Holiness comes wrapped in the ordinary. There are burning bushes all around you. Every tree is full of angels. Hidden beauty is waiting in every crumb. Life wants to lead you from crumbs to angels, but this can happen only if you are willing to unwrap the ordinary by staying with it long enough to harvest its treasure.*[4]
>
> — Macrina Wiederkehr

•10• What kinds of ordinary activities might hold unexpected treasures for you this week? Make an extra effort to be present in the moment and tune into "hidden beauty": a particularly lovely song from a bird outside your kitchen window; an unexpected pearl of wisdom from your child's lips; a word of kindness from a stranger.

•11• The first Saturday of each month, buy some fresh-cut flowers and enjoy them for the rest of the week. They will lift your spirits, especially on those cloudy, gray winter days.

•12• Adapt the following traditional African prayer in a way that fits your own surroundings. If you live in northern California, for instance, you might plug in giant redwoods for shady mango trees, the Sierra Nevadas for Mount Kilimanjaro. Celebrate the beauty around you, great and small.

All you big *things, bless the Lord.*
Mount Kilimanjaro and Lake Victoria,
The Rift Valley and the Serengeti Plain,
Fat baobabs and shady mango trees,
Bless the Lord.
Praise and extol Him for ever and ever.
All you tiny *things, bless the Lord.*
Busy black ants and hopping fleas,
Wriggling tadpoles and mosquito larvae,
Flying locusts and water drops,
Pollen dust and tsetse flies,
Millet seed and dried dagga,
Bless the Lord.
Praise and extol him for ever and ever.[5]

•13• Go to a playground you frequented as a child and spend some time "playing" — swing or slide, climb on the jungle gym, play catch, or shoot some hoops. Even better, take a childhood friend along and have a great time.

•14• Remember building elaborate forts out of blankets and your mother's dining room chairs? Or giving your dolls exciting and brilliant lives that captivated your imagination for hours at a time? Children are still the best teachers when it comes to turning mundane moments into great adventures. Next time a child asks you to play with him, do it instead of making an "adult" excuse. Enter into his world and leave your own behind.

•15• Go to a pet store or aquarium where you can observe a variety of tropical fish. Notice the difference in shapes, the brilliance of color, the diversity of expression.

•16• Spend some time in a museum or art gallery and *really look* at the works of art. Let the skill and imagination you see inspire your awe of the Master Artist whose creativity is imprinted on the soul of every human being.

> *Did you know that the artistic pattern on a giraffe's hide is as unique as a human being's fingerprints?*
>
> *Or that a six-ton elephant's trunk has more than 40,000 muscles that are strong enough to uproot a tree, yet sensitive enough to pick up a peanut?*

•17• Get a book or video about one of t great wonders in creation: the thriving wo beneath the sea, the power of an active v cano, the icy formations in Antarctica, prehistoric fossils of dinosaurs. Let you be stunned by the grandeur of it all.

•**18**• Do you know someone who possesses an especially playful spirit or childlike appreciation for life? If so, spend some time with that person and ask her how she cultivates an attitude of wonder.

•**19**• Make a list of five things you would love to do but haven't because you're "too old," "too busy," or "too scared." Pick one of these and do it despite your age, your busyness, or your fear. Watch your world expand.

•**20**• Where do you feel most sensually alive or spiritually inspired? On the peaceful shores of the Pacific? Atop a rugged mountain peak? In a grand cathedral? In your own rowboat on a trout-gorged lake? Make plans to visit a place that nurtures your soul. Put it on your calendar.

> *God does not die on the day we cease to believe in a personal deity, but we die on the day when our lives cease to be illuminated by the steady radiance, renewed daily, of a wonder, the source of which is beyond all reason.*[6]
>
> — DAG HAMMARSKJÖLD

•3•

TAKING A SPIRITUAL VACATION

Oh, that I had the wings of a dove!
I would fly away and be at rest.[1]
— King David

Who doesn't long for more time — that most precious and irreplaceable commodity — to rest, to draw inward, reflect, recuperate, and rejuvenate? Or, who doesn't at least *say* they long for that? Many of us make almost a litany of the lament "I never have enough time. . . ."

But when you do have a moment to yourself, what do you do with it? Flip on the TV? Call a friend? Read the newspaper? Play computer games? There is nothing wrong with any of these things, but if you find yourself saying you want more quiet time but are always *doing* something to fill it up, you may be sabotaging your spiritual life.

While we can't manufacture time, and there's a limited amount of it to spend, we can make more nourishing use of it than we often do. We can sit quietly for ten minutes;

we can take a drive into the mountains or schedule a whole weekend to retreat from our daily routines. We can take spiritual vacations.

We can. But will we?

Most of us aren't used to being alone with ourselves, much less alone with God. Distractions from rest, reflection, and prayer are as persistent as fussy children, as close as the computer mouse or ringing telephone. We complain about distractions, but we're comfortable with them. We're not as at home in the open spaces and quiet hallways of our souls. Few of us feel as safe with ourselves as we do in the company of our television sets.

Writer and minister Frederick Buechner describes the experience we all face when we venture into that private place within. "Part of the inner world of everyone," he says, "is this sense of emptiness, unease, incompleteness." But this disconcerting reality holds a sacred gift: "I believe that this in itself is a word from God, that this is the sound God's voice makes in a world that has explained him away. In such a world, I suspect that maybe God speaks to us most clearly through his silence, his absence, so that we may know him best through our missing him."[2]

Are you willing to dwell in your inner world for a while, to take a vacation from the frenetic and familiar and listen to the sound of God's voice? Sometimes spending time alone with ourselves and with God feels as unfamiliar as getting to know a new acquaintance; some moments can be a bit awkward, uncertain, even silent. But that's okay. If you're like most adults, you must *learn* to rest, retreat, refuel, and renew your acquaintance with yourself and with God. Once it may have come naturally, but you have forgotten how.

The good news is, taking a spiritual vacation is a choice you can make right now. You may not know exactly where you're going, but the trip will be rewarding. You need only begin.

Shouldn't we be able to keep up, to continue pitching as long as everybody and everything needs us? If we feel like hiding, aren't we weak-willed or irresponsible? No. To feel like hiding is to be human, to recognize the soul's desire to pull away and within, to respond to a need for replenishment. The problem is we don't hide often enough. If we practiced a periodic hiding, a repeated running away to God — often just for moments, sometimes for hours or days — we'd be less susceptible to letting the daily grind pulverize us.[3]

— JUDITH COUCHMAN

•1• Think about what kind of space your soul craves. Does it need a small, quiet closet to hide in? A bright room full of soft pillows to lounge in? A rugged mountaintop swallowed in endless sky to stretch in? Draw a simple picture of your ideal "space" (with you in it) and carry it with you to remind you it's as close as your imagination.

•2• When the radio or television is blaring, it can be difficult to hear someone speak. It's the same in our spiritual life. This week, find one way to dial down your personal internal radio — the distractions of daily life that drown out the still, small voice speaking to your heart. Cancel an evening meeting in favor of a few hours of reading and reflecting. You can sit before a blazing fire or enjoy a relaxing bath. It doesn't matter what you do to create a quiet space — just do it.

•3• What is the common denominator of vacations? A break from routine. Think of small ways you can break from your routine this week. Walk to work, have a picnic dinner with your family on a blanket in the living room, go for a run instead of to the gym. Use a change in activity to pay attention to your soul and what it needs to thrive.

> *As soon as we are alone, without people to talk with, books to read, TV to watch, or phone calls to make, an inner chaos opens up in us. This chaos can be so disturbing and so confusing that we can hardly wait to get busy again. Entering a private room and shutting the door, therefore, does not mean that we immediately shut out all our inner doubts, anxieties, fears, bad memories, unresolved conflicts, angry feelings, and impulsive desires.*[4]
>
> — HENRI NOUWEN

•4• Try eating a meal by yourself in silence, without anything to read, listen to, or watch on TV. Think about the ways God has shown love to you and your family this week. Express your gratitude. When the "inner chaos" opens up inside you, thank God for being bigger than any problem you have today.

•5• Take yourself to a beautiful place for a private picnic lunch. Sit on a blanket under a tree, or lean back in the seat in your car if it's cold. Don't distract yourself with anything — just enjoy the view and relax.

•6• Give yourself a half-day retreat as a birthday gift each year. Use the time to focus on your dreams and goals. Make a list of anything and everything you would like to accomplish in the next several years. Then prioritize the list into one-year, three-year, and five-year dreams. Allow yourself to think about activities, interests, skills, and experiences that would add depth and richness to your life. Formulate a plan of action and review the list every year to see how your dreams are unfolding. Stay open to a divine change of plans.

So often we think, Okay, now I've got to run around to get what I need. I've got to go to the mountains of Tibet or to a magical island in Hawaii. I've got to go someplace *to begin this spiritual journey. But the fact is, the moment we say we want to go on that journey, we've begun it — right where we are.*[5]

— MELODY BEATTIE

•7• Take five minutes to go on a mini-vacation in your imagination. Close your eyes and let a picture come into your mind of a "getaway" spot you'd love to go to — a place that is peaceful and rejuvenating to your spirit.

•8• Next time you're in a stressful situation, see if you can remove yourself, even for a few minutes. As soon as you're away from the situation, travel to your peaceful spot and rest your spirit. Take some deep breaths and ask for divine guidance before you go back into the fray. You may be surprised at how much easier it is to resolve problems and tensions after you take a moment's break.

•9• Make a list of at least ten activities that rejuvenate you emotionally and spiritually. Write one into your schedule each week.

•10• Reserve a small room or corner of a room in your house as your "quiet corner." Clear it of clutter, add a candle, a comfortable pillow or chair, something beautiful for the wall, a few good books, and then savor it as your personal refuge — a place to be still, to ponder and pour out your heart to God — far from the madding crowd.

> *A constituted place stands there beckoning to us, reminding us to make the time. Probably very few will be able to use a whole room in their home exclusively as a place for apartness, for prayer and solitude. For most, the at-home place apart may well have to be an alcove, a dormer, a closet, a corner of [a] room. To each his own. The important thing is that there is this place which, when one goes there, even if the going is no more than turning one's chair around, one has a sense of having gone apart. If one cannot find such a niche anywhere at home, then one has to look farther afield, perhaps a nearby church or chapel. One might find a park, a library, a museum. A businessman might create his prayer corner in his office. A car has been a hermitage for many.*[6]
>
> — M. Basil Pennington

•**11**• Some wise soul has remarked that "even an angel can't do two things at once." Some cooks, for instance, find it hard to converse with guests and prepare a meal at the same time. Use your time away from the hurly-burly to focus on a nagging concern that never gets your undivided attention. Listen to what's bothering you and then imagine yourself sitting down with someone entirely wise and loving to discuss it. What advice do you hear?

•**12**• Once a year, schedule a whole weekend for silent retreat. Check out monasteries or other retreat centers in your area and make a reservation for your soul. Take along inspirational books, a journal, your hiking shoes.

•**13**• Brother Lawrence, the author of the classic *The Practice of the Presence of God*, used to imagine himself as a stone before a sculptor. Set aside five minutes each morning for one week, asking the divine Artist to imprint his image on your soul, just as a sculptor shaping stone. Then consider whatever happens to you that week and in the months ahead as God's chisel, perfecting a living work of art.

[The] "resting of God" on the seventh day [of creation] became the theological framework for the Sabbath regulation that summons us to rest in God. Now, before we dismiss this Old Testament rule out of hand, it is important to see that there is a lot more behind it than the desire for a periodic breather. For instance, it has a way of tempering our gnawing need to always get ahead. If we ever want to know the degree to which we are enslaved by the passion to possess, all we have to do is observe the difficulty we have maintaining a Sabbath rhythm.[7]

— RICHARD J. FOSTER

•14• What are you afraid you'll miss out on if you take a "vacation" from your regular routine? How many of these things have to do with your ego? Be honest!

•15• Take a few minutes to reflect on the week just past. What did you do with your free time? Did it rejuvenate you spiritually? Take note of what you want to repeat in the week ahead, or what you want to change.

•16• One evening a month, have a date with yourself. Hire a baby-sitter and go someplace special: a quiet café, your favorite bookstore, an art gallery. Spend time nurturing yourself in quiet ways.

•17• After the kids are in bed and your day's activities are winding down, turn off all the noise in your home, turn out the lights, light a candle, and sit upright in a chair or cross-legged on the floor. Breathe slowly, concentrating on each breath, relaxing each muscle in your body one at a time. Even if you can't relax, remain sitting for at least ten minutes. With practice, you will learn to slow down the chatter in your mind and make a still space within where God can speak to you, or just soothe you.

> *Come to Me, all who are weary and heavy-laden, and I will give you rest. Take My yoke upon you, and learn from Me, for I am gentle and humble in heart; and you shall find rest for your souls. For My yoke is easy, and My load is light.*[8]
>
> — Jesus Christ

•18• Set aside one Saturday a month to celebrate a "Sabbath" meal. Let it be the beginning of a twenty-four-hour period of spiritual rejuvenation, a time to connect with God as well as with family and friends. Begin the meal by lighting a candle that can safely burn through the evening and the next day, and pray this prayer as you light it:

Blessed are you, Lord our God, King of the Universe, who gives us joy as we kindle the Sabbath light.

Then pass around a loaf of home-baked bread, inviting each person to break off a piece. Pray this prayer:

The eyes of all look to you, O Lord, and you give them their food in due season.
You open your hand, you satisfy the desire of every living thing.
Blessed are you, Lord our God, King of the Universe, who brings forth bread from the earth.

After that, share a delicious meal and enjoy the evening as God's gift to you and your loved ones.

•19• Use the Sunday following your "Sabbath" meal to enjoy simple pleasures — playing games with the kids, visiting friends, writing letters, reading a good book. Resist the urge to run to the mall, settle in front of the TV, or open your briefcase.

•20• Mark eight days on your calendar to meditate on these words from the Sermon on the Mount, traditionally known as the Beatitudes, taken from *The Message*, a contemporary rendering of the Bible:

DAY ONE: "You're blessed when you're at the end of your rope. With less of you there is more of God."

DAY TWO: "You're blessed when you feel you've lost what is most dear to you. Only then can you be embraced by the One most dear to you."

DAY THREE: "You're blessed when you're content with just who you are — no more, no less."

DAY FOUR: "You're blessed when you've worked up a good appetite for God. He's food and drink in the best meal you'll ever eat."

DAY FIVE: "You're blessed when you care. At the moment of being 'care-full,' you find yourselves cared for."

DAY SIX: "You're blessed when you get your inside world — your mind and your heart — put right. Then you can see God in the outside world."

DAY SEVEN: "You're blessed when you can show people how to cooperate instead of compete or fight."

DAY EIGHT: "You're blessed when your commitment to God provokes persecution. The persecution drives you even deeper into God's kingdom."[9]

Each day, write the beatitude for that day on an index card and carry it with you to refer to during the quiet moments in between activities. If any insights come to mind about how the beatitude can be applied in your life, jot them down.

We do not all have the flexibility in our lives to be able to make the time and establish the space for a weekly day of apartness. But, let's be very realistic here. There is in the lives of most of us a good bit more freedom and flexibility to organize such a dimension, if we really want to. Do I really want time apart? Do I know I need time apart? I do make time and place for what I want, what I need.[10]

— M. Basil Pennington

•4•

HEALING YOUR SOUL

Your willingness to wrestle with your demons will cause your angels to sing. Use the pain as fuel, as a reminder of your strength.[1]

— AUGUST WILSON

Do you ever feel stagnant? At times in your life, it may feel like nothing you do to nourish your soul makes any difference. When you think about God or spiritual things, you may feel heavy. Sad. Even angry. You may long for spiritual vitality and peace but feel confused and weary instead.

When we feel spiritually dormant — even dead — or the mere thought of God and our souls makes us cringe somewhere deep inside, there is a reason. Perhaps it's been so long since we've paid any serious attention to our spiritual life that approaching the Creator of the Universe makes us feel guilty or frightened. Maybe we've dishonored God or our own soul through thoughts or actions we regret, and we're just not sure how to clear away the wreckage. We might be fed up with the difficulties of life and cynical about how God is involved in a world where suffering is par for the course. Or our soul may be nursing a deep wound that we think no one else, not even God, can possibly understand.

A soul that is sick or injured cannot assimilate nourishment as well as a healthy soul can. Part of the spiritual journey for all of us involves recognizing the ways in which our souls have been sullied or wounded and gently opening them to cleansing and healing.

Think of a time when you felt especially alive spiritually, especially hungry for and satisfied by your experience of God. What was going on in your life? What were you doing to nourish your soul? Where were you getting your inspiration? What was your internal picture of God?

Think about where you are today. Consider things you've experienced between then and now that may have drained your spiritual vitality. Did something or someone tear at the threads of your faith? Did you have a fight with God? Did life puncture your soul so deeply that you wonder how you will ever recover?

Sometimes things happen that make us question the goodness of life, the worth of our being, the wisdom of the Universe, the very essence of God. Sometimes guilt or anger or hurt or fear bind our souls so tightly that spiritual breath and movement become impossible.

Has your soul been wounded? Has it crawled off into a corner to bleed or mourn? Has it taken cover like a soldier in a sealed battle tank? Is it aching for the soothing reassurance that all is well, that Love prevails?

Removing the protective coverings from your soul is scary. It feels risky. Why should you do it? Because it's so very quiet and lonely in hiding. It's so empty without hope. Suffering that lacks context and meaning can be deadly. Your wounds just get deeper.

Consider coming out into the light. Bring your battered heart or your shaking fist or your trembling spirit right into the center of your life. Dare to raise the curtain. Let God see you exactly as you are. God can handle it. So can you.

Beyond the splendors of the soul there is also a darkness dangerous to deny. Something essential in us steals — or is stolen — away, leaving emptiness, alienation, or pain in the core of our being where we know there was once something full and vital. There is a hole where once was soul. The crisis seizes us when we're in the steely grip of grief, betrayal, physical terror, numbing routine, or an inauthentic life.[2]

— SCOTT COUSINEAU

•1• Which of these do you most identify with: a battered heart, a shaking fist, or a trembling spirit? Write a couple of paragraphs about your experience with one or all of them. Better yet, talk about it with someone you trust.

•2• Psychologists have discovered that writing with the left hand (or the right if we're left-handed) may reveal thoughts and feelings of which we are unaware. It may be that the childlike side of us, writing in crude scrawl, is more honest than the adult, who tries to be articulate or "correct." With a pencil or crayon, write a few sentences about something that is bothering you. Do the words tell you anything you didn't know?

•3• In the most loving, reassuring voice you can manage, write a response to the honest words you have just put down. You may be surprised at the wisdom, strength, and faith hidden deep inside you.

> *Sometimes, if I become* de-*pressed, it's usually because I need to* ex-*press something. We all have paintings and music and writing inside of us. Keep supplies close at hand: brushes, pens, giant boxes of crayons, paints and pads of paper — the tools of expression.*[3]
>
> — SARK

•4• Think of someone who has hurt you very deeply. What feelings come up when you think of this person and what he or she did? If you have a box of crayons or watercolors, try to draw or paint those feelings. When your "picture" is finished, create another one that expresses what your soul would look like if those hurts were healed.

•5• The "Big Book" of Alcoholics Anonymous (AA) states that "resentment is the 'number one' offender. From it stem all forms of spiritual disease."[4] In the Fourth Step of AA, recovering alcoholics are encouraged to list people, institutions, or principles with whom they are angry. Then they ask themselves why they are angry, probing honestly to discover how their own self-interest may have set them up to be hurt. Get the book *Alcoholics Anonymous* and take yourself through this "Fourth Step" process in Chapter 5. See if you learn anything new about the causes of your pain or what might help you heal.

•6• If you're mad at God, you're not the first person to feel that way. Thousands of years ago, a man named Job railed at God with these words: "I am weary of living. Let me complain freely. I will speak my sorrow and bitterness. I will say to God, 'Don't just condemn me — tell me *why* you are doing it. Does it really seem right to you to oppress and despise me, a man you have made? Are you unjust like men?' "[5]

Write your own "letter" to God, telling him *exactly* how you feel. Read it to him out loud. Then sit quietly for at least ten minutes and write down anything you hear from him in response. If you don't hear anything, ask him to open your ears; then put your letter away and go about your business. You may hear from him later in a quiet or powerful way.

•7• Read the entire Old Testament story of Job's experience with suffering and his agonizing battle with God. Mark the verses you particularly identify with, or insights you get into your own life.

> *Most assume that trust is quiet, serene, selfless dependence on God. Though there is an element of truth to that view of trust, more often than not such serene faith is a byproduct of wanting very little from God. It is frighteningly easy to appear trusting when in fact one is simply dead (in denial of the wounds, hunger, or struggle of the heart). Genuine trust involves allowing another to matter and have an impact on our lives. For that reason, many who hate and do battle with God trust Him more deeply than those whose complacent faith permits an abstract and motionless stance before Him. Those who trust God most are those whose faith permits them to risk wrestling with Him over the deepest questions of life. Good hearts are captured in a divine wrestling match; fearful, doubting hearts stay clear of the mat.*[6]
>
> — DAN B. ALLENDER

•8• Reflect on a past hurt or trauma that no longer causes you intense pain, fear, or anger. What helped you heal?

•9• Think of people you know or know about who have experienced major losses or heartaches. Which ones seem bitter or "stuck" because of them? Which ones seem to have grown through them or have meaning and joy in their lives in spite of them? Spend some time reflecting on what you think makes the difference between these two groups of people.

•10• Who do you know who deals with pain, loss, or injustice in a way you admire? Ask this person to share their experience and wisdom with you, and listen for keys to serenity that you can apply in your life. If you feel comfortable sharing a specific struggle you're having, ask this wise guide for advice on how you could look at it differently or deal with it more constructively.

> *Narrow is the mansion of my soul; let it be enlarged that you may enter. It is in ruins; do repair it. It has within it what must offend your eyes; I confess it and know it. But who shall cleanse it? To whom should I cry except to you?*[7]
>
> — St. Augustine

•11• Guilt is a soul-crippling affliction. Shame is even worse. Is there something you've done that makes you feel guilty, or something you *are* that causes you shame? Next time you're near a deep lake, river, or ocean, pick up a rock and, using your imagination, "attach" your guilt or shame to it. Then throw it as far as you can into the water. As it sinks, open your soul to God's forgiveness and unconditional love.

•12• Write on small slips of paper words or phrases that represent the major resentments, regrets, or fears in your life. One at a time, tear up or burn each slip of paper in a symbolic act of surrender.

•13• If there is a soul-numbing resentment, regret, or fear you "can't" let go of, ask yourself why. What are you getting out of holding on to it?

•14• If you knew you were going to die tomorrow, what broken or hurting relationship would you wish could be healed before you leave this earth — your relationship with a parent or child, a special friend, your spouse, yourself, God? Write down what is stopping you from moving toward healing today, then ask God for advice on how you can get moving.

Celebration is possible only through the deep realization that life and death are never found completely separate. Celebration can really come about only where fear and love, joy and sorrow, tears and smiles can exist together. Celebration is the acceptance of life in a constantly increasing awareness of its preciousness. And life is precious not only because it can be seen, touched, and tasted, but also because it will be gone one day. We can indeed make all our sorrows, just as much as our joys, a part of our celebration of life in the deep realization that life and death are not opponents but do, in fact, kiss each other at every moment of our existence.[8]

— HENRI NOUWEN

•15• Are there parts of yourself you have rejected because they cause you shame or suffering? Have you "banished" something about yourself that needs to be cleansed or embraced in order for you to be at peace? Have a "welcoming" ceremony for that part of yourself. Invite God to the ceremony and ask him how he would have you deal with your shame or suffering.

•16• Remember when your mother dabbed alcohol into a small scrape or cut when you were little? You winced and maybe even cried out at the sting of its cleansing power. Think about a time in your life when pain was a necessary precursor to healing. Let that memory encourage you to endure whatever it takes to become cleansed and whole again. May the words of the psalmist David comfort you: "The LORD is close to the brokenhearted and saves those who are crushed in spirit."[9]

•17• Poet Luci Shaw says, "The longer I live, the more I realize that the greatest pain is often the place of greatest growth."[10] Think of at least three painful experiences in your past that resulted in significant personal growth. Write down some specific lessons you learned or blessings you received. Then, in faith, tell God you trust him to bring invaluable growth out of whatever circumstance is causing you pain today.

•18• It's natural to want to deny or run from feelings and thoughts that make us uncomfortable. Next time you feel like running, defy your natural instinct and turn instead to face whatever is going on inside you. Try saying out loud, with gentleness, "Welcome, fear. Hello, bitter memory. What do you want to say to me?" Then listen.

It is impossible to remove oneself totally from suffering, unless one removes oneself from life itself, no longer enters into relationships, makes oneself invulnerable. Contrary to what one might wish, pain, losses, amputations, are part of even the smoothest life one can imagine.[11]

— DOROTHEE SOLLE

•19• It has been said that "we're as sick as our secrets." If you carry a secret that is making your soul sick or is keeping you from a peaceful, joyful life, get rid of it. Muster up all your courage, and ask a trusted friend, a member of the clergy, or a counselor to hear your "confession." Make sure to choose someone who will not shame you, but will help you heal.

•20• Take five minutes before you climb into bed to review the past twenty-four hours. Reflect on the challenges, the joys, the frustrations, the opportunities. Give thanks for the whole ball of wax. Ask God's forgiveness for any failures or regrets. Lie down in peace and sleep well.

We walk in darkness, risking bruising ourselves against a thousand obstacles. But we know that "God is Love" and trust in God as our light. I have the feeling that what is asked of us is to live in the whirlwind, without keeping back anything for ourselves — in fact to let ourselves pitch and toss in the waves of divine will till the day when it will say: "That is enough."[12]

— Raissa Maritain

•5•

SOUL FOOD

How many a man has dated a new era in his life from the reading of a book![1]
— HENRY DAVID THOREAU

What have you watched, read, and listened to this week? Start with today. If you're an average urban dweller, the first input of your day may have been a blast of sound from your clock radio. You may have listened to a morning news show or drive-time banter and snarfed down the headlines along with your cereal. By midday you probably processed several more memos or e-mail messages or bills or recipes. And by evening you haven't even started on the work you brought home, the program on public television, the Web surfing, or the novel you've been wanting to get back to since last weekend.

Meanwhile, your soul is growling like an empty stomach. When was the last time you gave it a really good meal?

We live in the Information Age, yet suffer from spiritual impoverishment. Our souls can't grow strong and wise on the steady diet of pabulum we usually feed them. We need something different. We need solid soul food.

Webster's defines solid as "not hollow; having three dimensions; firm; strong; substantial; reliable or dependable." What are the tangible things you depend on to nourish your soul? What spiritual meal leaves you feeling satisfied?

Whatever you take in through your ears and eyes dishes up something for your soul. If you rarely see or hear anything but the cacophony of stimuli that bombards you in a typical day, you'll starve spiritually. You need to make a concerted effort to root out the soul food that nourishes you and build it into your daily diet.

There are myriad entrees on the menu:

- a book that challenges you with its insight
- a painting, sculpture, or photograph that touches a nerve deep inside you
- a musical score that transports you with its beauty or rhythm
- a lecture that teaches you to think more deeply
- a conversation with a soulmate about what really matters
- a hymn that becomes a prayer when you sing it

- a poem whose cadence and craftsmanship is balm to your soul
- a view that takes your breath away
- a communion with nature that fills up your senses.

Improving your spiritual diet doesn't have to be complicated, laborious, or even terribly time-consuming. With a little attention and effort you can satisfy the parts of you that are the most important and probably most hungry. Won't it feel good to eat a real meal?

> *Books can speak to us like God, like men or like the noise of the city we live in. They speak to us like God when they bring us light and peace and fill us with silence. They speak to us like the noise of the city when they hold us captive by a weariness that tells us nothing, give us no peace, and no support, nothing to remember, and yet will not let us escape. Books that speak like the noise of multitudes reduce us to despair by the sheer weight of their emptiness. They entertain us like the lights of the city streets at night, by hopes they cannot fulfil.*[2]
>
> — THOMAS MERTON

•1• In the past year, have you read a book that spoke to you "like God"? If so, recommend it to someone else this week. Then ask at least five people you know to recommend a book that might feed your soul.

•2• If you need extra ideas, try reading one or more of the following books in the year ahead:

The Cloister Walk by Kathleen Norris
Windows of the Soul by Ken Gire
A Grace Disguised by Gerald Sittser
Pilgrim at Tinker Creek by Annie Dillard
The Book of God by Walter Wangerin
Soul Making by Alan Jones
The Inner Voice of Love by Henri Nouwen
The Way of the Heart by Henri Nouwen
Glittering Images by Susan Howatch
In the Beginning by Chaim Potok
Till We Have Faces by C. S. Lewis
The Divine Romance by Gene Edwards
Bright Flows the River by Taylor Caldwell
Stones from the River by Ursula Hegi

•3• Join or start a reading group that focuses on spiritually nourishing books. Once a month you will experience the pleasure and challenge of talking with others who are focusing on their spiritual journey.

Who would call a day spent reading a good day? But a life spent reading — that's a good life.[3]

— ANNIE DILLARD

•4• If you spend much time commuting, consider buying or borrowing some books on tape. Make those hours in transit work *for* rather than against your soul.

•5• Make a pact with a friend to dig up one inspiring, challenging, or comforting quote every week and share it with each other. Even just a handful of thought-provoking words from someone wise can nourish your soul for the day.

•6• Invite a few friends for pizza, chitchat, and a movie on video. Make sure they're folks who are comfortable discussing spiritual and relational things. Watch any of the following videos and then take a half hour afterward to discuss the movie and its impact on you:

Chariots of Fire
Schindler's List
Babette's Feast
Moll Flanders
The Mission

The Shawshank Redemption
At Play in the Fields of the Lord
Strangers in Good Company
To Kill a Mockingbird
The Doctor
The Joy Luck Club
Shadowlands
Phenomenon
The Spitfire Grill
Jerry Maguire

•7• Watch your local newspaper for notices of upcoming lectures on topics you think might stretch or feed your soul. Watch for the same on public television and make a night of it.

> *Become an active creator of your own sound environment, rather than being at the mercy of every hammering rock video and grating aspirin commercial that invades your quieter moments. You need not be a slave to the stresses of our high-tech society. If you feel tense and harried, you can release that tension with just a few minutes of calming music. If you are depressed, you don't need to stay depressed. A short sound-bath in certain kinds of music will lift you out of your depression. You may find in the music a friend and companion, an inner voice that seems to sense what you need and which path you should take, a Divine Presence that lets you know you are being protected and guided.*[4]
>
> — STEPHANIE MERRITT

•**8**• Buy one of the popular Gregorian chant tapes or CDs. (The Benedictine Monks of Santo Domingo de Silos have recorded one called *Chant* on the Angel label.) Leave it on as background music for your day. See if you feel any more relaxed or centered than usual at day's end.

•**9**• Find fifteen minutes of solitude and listen to a recording of Samuel Barber's "Adagio for Strings" or Ralph Vaughan Williams's

"Fantasia on a Theme by Thomas Tallis" or "5 Variants of 'Dives and Lazarus.' " If you have stereo headphones, listen through them with your eyes closed. Enter into the depth of emotion and passion of the composer — and of the Composer behind the composer.

•10• Tune in to how you're feeling and choose a piece of recorded music that fits your mood. If you're melancholy, listen to slow, sad music for a while. If you're energetic, turn up a march or rock selection. See if you agree with Stephanie Merritt, who said, "By suggesting sorrow, joy, or anger, music stirs our emotions and gives us 'permission' to feel and express them."[5]

> *Music seems to induce a heightened empathy with others, a sense of unity among people and things, a sensitivity for the divine. It can lead you to ineffable experiences of grandeur and beauty.*[6]
>
> — HELEN L. BONNY AND LOUIS M. SAVARY

•11• If your community has a "sing-along *Messiah,*" sing along next Christmas season. Take some friends with you.

•12• If you play an instrument, spend an hour

one evening a week making music that feeds your soul. Better yet, involve your family or friends in a "band" or sing-along.

•**13**• Check out some books from your local library that feature the paintings of some of the masters: Renoir, Pissarro, Rembrandt, Corot. . . . Spend an evening poring over their masterpieces with some soothing music in the background and your favorite beverage at your side.

> *Art's a staple. Like bread or wine or a warm coat in winter. Those who think it is a luxury have only a fragment of a mind. Man's spirit grows hungry for art in the same way his stomach growls for food.*[7]
>
> — IRVING STONE

•**14**• Attend an opening at a local art gallery. Regardless of what kind of art is showing, take time to learn about each artist's unique themes and techniques. Enjoy being among other people who appreciate art and who have chosen to spend time looking at it instead of at their television screens.

•**15**• Keep your eyes open for a children's art exhibit. Or even better, pay close attention to your own child's artistic endeavors. Let the unbridled creativity of a young soul touch and delight your own.

•16• Whether you consider yourself artistic or not, you are gifted with your own unique way of expressing yourself. Choose an artistic medium — paint or pencil, song or instrument, design or construction — and make something with your hands. Put your whole soul into it.

•17• Take a pottery or sculpting class and experience the fun of creating something out of a shapeless piece of clay. Dare to step outside the norm and create something in the shape of your own soul. If clay doesn't appeal to you, try ceramics, watercolors, or wood carving. Express yourself!

> *The world of today is sick to its thin blood for lack of elemental things, for fire before the hands, for water welling from the earth, for air, for the dear earth itself underneath.*[8]
>
> — HENRY BESTON

•18• For most of us, God feels more real when we're surrounded by the most magnificent example of his creativity and majesty. But you don't have to wait for a trip to the wilds to experience the soul-enriching connection with nature. Think of one way you can commune with nature this week — be it as simple as breathing deeply on a frosty morning, dipping your toes in a pond, or digging in the dirt of your garden.

•19• Follow the example of Eugene Peterson, who talks about how creation nourishes his life with God: "I took a walk this morning down to the beach. I do this two or three times a week. In the early morning I usually have the place to myself. I sit on a piece of driftwood and take in the world of mountain and water, sky and weather. And the birds, I watch and admire the birds: goldeneyes, buffleheads, usually a great blue heron, mallards, gulls, ravens, and an occasional bald eagle. The intricate intersections of beauty make a fine warp for my prayers."[9]

•20• Take fifteen minutes to ponder this prayer by poet Edna St. Vincent Millay: "God, I can push the grass apart and lay my finger on Thy heart."[10] What are some specific things you have learned about God from your personal experience with nature? Commit yourself to being observant so you'll recognize what nature might have to teach you in the month ahead.

I meant to do my work to-day —
But a brown bird sang in the appletree,
And a butterfly flitted across the field,
And all the leaves were calling me.

And the wind went sighing over the land,
Tossing the grasses to and fro,
And a rainbow held out its shining hand —
So what could I do but laugh and go?[11]

— RICHARD LE GALLIENNE

•6•

SOUL TALK

When we begin working on our own souls, we discover that we are not self-made. Our identity depends on Another.[1]

— ALAN JONES

Do you ever talk to yourself? Do you have conversations in your head with a whole committee of folks who want to give you their opinion? If you're like most people, your mind can get awfully full of voices. Some may be helpful and soothing, but most just make a lot of noise. Your own may be the loudest — and most unfriendly — of all.

The fact is, the soul does not thrive in the limited space of Self. While we need time to be just with ourselves, to meander physically and mentally, we also need communion and direction on a higher plane. Apart from interaction with the divine, the soul merely talks to itself. Eventually that gets boring. Sometimes it's downright destructive. And ultimately it depletes us spiritually. We're just not big enough to carry the whole world on our shoulders without sharing our burdens and joys with Someone greater than ourselves.

A song written by the Hebrew psalmist David points to the nature of humankind. On one hand, we're so very finite and insignificant:

I look up at your macro-skies, dark and
enormous, your handmade sky-jewelry,
Moon and stars mounted in their settings.
Then I look at my micro-self and wonder,
Why do you bother with us?
Why take a second look our way?

On the other hand, the Creator has given us a place of honor in the scheme of things:

Yet we've so narrowly missed being gods,
bright with Eden's dawn light.
You put us in charge of your handcrafted
world, repeated to us your Genesis-charge,
Made us lords of sheep and cattle,
even animals out in the wild,
Birds flying and fish swimming,
whales singing in the ocean depths.[2]

David sings the paradox: We have a special place in the universe, but we are not omnipotent. We are not all-wise or self-sufficient. We need direction, support, guidance, relief, and love from outside of ourselves. And we need it from Someone who is bigger than all of us.

Walter Wink goes so far as to say, "What we need is a portable form of the Wailing Wall in Jerusalem, where we can unburden ourselves of accumulated suffering. We must not try to bear the sufferings of the creation ourselves. We are to articulate these agonizing longings and let them pass through us to God. Only the heart of the loving God can endure such a weight of suffering. Our attempts to bear them (and our depression is evidence that we try) are masochistic, falsely messianic, and finally idolatrous, as if there were no God, as if we had to carry this burden all by ourselves."[3]

We don't have to. Even if conversing with the divine sometimes seems like talking to ourselves — or to a brick wall — we will do well to practice it. Call it prayer; call it lament, supplication, or intercession. Call it talking to God. Just do it. Invite God in for conversation. It's much more interesting than listening to your internal voices bounce off the walls of your mind. You might even learn something . . . or meet Someone.

The value of persistent prayer is not that he will hear us . . . but that we will finally hear him.[4]

— WILLIAM MCGILL

•1• In your opinion, what is the purpose of prayer? If you think it is of any importance, write a paragraph explaining why. Sometimes knowing why we're doing something helps us stick with it.

•2• What place has prayer and meditation held in your life through the years? Write down at least five reasons why you either have or have not made it a regular practice. What does your list tell you about your perception of yourself and of God?

•3• Rebecca Manley Pippert uncovers the attitude some of us have toward addressing the divine: "Sometimes we expect God to hop to, secretly feeling he is lucky even to have us consider him."[5] Spend a few moments honestly assessing your own attitude toward God and prayer. In what ways have you approached God as though he is a cosmic vending machine? Consider how these words of Phillips Brooks might affect your prayer posture: "Prayer is not conquering

God's reluctance, but taking hold of God's willingness."[6]

Prayer is not a way to get things from God, but so that we may get to know God. Prayer is not to be used as the privilege of a spoiled child seeking ideal conditions to indulge his spiritual propensities; the purpose of prayer is to reveal the presence of God.[7]

— OSWALD CHAMBERS

•4• When you think about the activity of talking to God, what are the first thoughts and feelings that come to mind? Where is God in the picture? Where are you? Try drawing a simple picture of what you see. Does this exercise tell you anything about why prayer is either easy or hard for you?

•5• If talking and listening to God is not something you're used to doing, it may feel awkward, scary, boring, or downright pointless. Don't let your misgivings stop you from opening the door to communicating with an invisible Being beyond yourself. You may find that "going through the motions" will yield surprising results.

•6• Light several candles, each representing

a specific area of your life. Take a few moments to pray about each area, blowing out the corresponding candle as you go. When all is dark, sit for at least five minutes and listen for anything God might have to say to you.

> *We yearn for prayer and hide from prayer. We are attracted to it and repelled by it. We believe prayer is something we should do, even something we want to do, but it seems like a chasm stands between us and actually praying.*
>
> *We experience the agony of prayerlessness. We are not quite sure what holds us back. Of course we are busy with work and family obligations, but that is only a smoke screen. Our busyness seldom keeps us from eating or sleeping or making love. No, there is something deeper, more profound keeping us in check.*[8]
>
> — RICHARD J. FOSTER

•7• List the five things you most want or need. Take five days this week to pray about each. Listen for what God has to say to you about each thing on your list. If you receive any guidance about action you need to take, take it. God often works in partnership with us to bring what we need into our lives.

•8• A wise soul has said, "As the doubter tries the process of prayer, he should begin to add up the results. If he persists, he will almost surely find more serenity, more tolerance, less fear, and less anger. The idea that he may have been hypnotizing himself by autosuggestion will become laughable."[9] If you doubt the power of prayer, start keeping a notebook of your prayers and their results. A year from now, you may find your faith has increased.

•9• Make a prayer list for each day of the week. Include the situations and people you want to focus on regularly. Post the list on your bathroom mirror, tape it on the dashboard of your car, or tuck it into the latest mystery novel on your nightstand. Then spend five or ten minutes a day praying about what is on your list.

•10• On a day you plan to be at home or at your desk most of the day, set a timer to alert you once an hour. Stop for a few minutes and send up a short prayer for something or someone on your list.

> *Prayer is exhaling the spirit of man and inhaling the spirit of God.*[10]
>
> — Edwin Keith

•11• Sit up straight and close your eyes. Breathe deeply several times until your breathing settles into a slow, steady rhythm. On your next exhalation, consciously release something you're worrying about, considering, or planning. Whatever is on your internal agenda, breathe it out. As you inhale, ask God for his wisdom, clarity, and love, and then imagine you're breathing those things in. Continue this until you feel more at peace.

•12• Next time you find yourself worrying or obsessing about a situation or person, say (out loud, if you can), STOP! Then immediately take your concern to God and tell him all about it.

•13• Gather a handful of stones, each one representing a concern you have right now. Go somewhere solitary and quiet and throw each stone as far as you can while saying out loud: "God, I let go of _________ and give it to you." Every time the same concerns come back into your mind, recall the moment you surrendered them to Someone more powerful than you.

> *Every happening, great and small, is a parable whereby God speaks to us, and the art of life is to get the message.*[11]
>
> — MALCOLM MUGGERIDGE

•14• Think back through the past year, looking specifically for events that may have held a message for you. Write down anything that comes to mind, and consider whether you need to take action regarding something God has been teaching you. Thank God for the way he communicates through people and circumstances, and pledge to keep your spiritual eyes and ears open today.

•15• Next time you arrive early for an appointment or are left waiting by a tardy client or friend, use the time creatively and spiritually. Rather than reading or stewing or fuming, spend the time praying for the person you're waiting for. Let those prayers prompt others for friends, relatives, or the waiter serving your coffee.

•16• American poet Ralph Waldo Emerson said, "Prayer is the contemplation of the facts of life from the highest point of view."[12] Take twenty minutes away from distractions to contemplate a situation that's bothering or challenging you, asking for wisdom. Then make some notes of any new perspectives or solutions that came to mind.

•17• Read some of the heartfelt prayers in the book of Psalms in the Old Testament. (Suggestions: Psalms 3, 6, 13, 18, 22, 27, 63). Then try writing your own psalm that reflects where you are in your life right now.

> *For me, prayer is an upward leap of the heart, an untroubled glance toward heaven, a cry of gratitude and love which I utter from the depths of sorrow as well as from the heights of joy. It has a supernatural grandeur that expands the soul and unites it with God.*[13]
>
> — THÉRÈSE OF LISIEUX

•18• Sometimes our physical posture can help us pray more consciously and fervently. Try kneeling when you pray, or even lying prostrate in humble reverence and surrender. Or lift your face and hands to heaven in supplication or joyous praise.

•19• One day this month skip breakfast and lunch and drink only fruit juice and water throughout the day. Make it a special day of conversation between you and God. Tell him you are hungrier for him than you are for food.

•20• Even brief prayers to begin and end the day are better than no prayer at all. Think of them as spiritual bookends, blessing all the hours that lie between. Try this prayer morning and evening. Given by Moses to the Israelites in the Hebrew Scriptures, it is a prayer Jews call the *Shema:*

> *Hear, O Israel: The Lord our God, the Lord is one. Love the Lord your God with all your heart and with all your soul and with all your strength. These commandments that I give you today are to be upon your hearts. Impress them on your children. Talk about them when you sit at home and when you walk along the road, when you lie down and when you get up. Tie them as symbols on your hands and bind them on your foreheads. Write them on the doorframes of your houses and on your gates.*[14]

•7•

SOULMATES

Community is the circle that embraces us, the safety net. Community is the line that connects us, the heart line. We bond in relationship and through these relationships give birth to spiritual community.[1]

— NELLY KAUFER AND CAROL OSMER-NEWHOUSE

According to the Hebrew book of Genesis, the Creator of humankind took into account a profound human need when he declared: "It isn't good for man to be alone; I will make a companion for him."[2]

We are not designed to travel through life in single file. Our goal on this earth is not to reach a spiritual nirvana where we commune only with God and no longer need our fellow human beings. We are meant to reach out and embrace a community of souls. A Jewish teacher explains that the essence of the Torah is development of intimacy with all things. "Even in the furthest reaches of enlightenment, even in the furthest reaches of the Infinite, there is the personal. The personal exists in community and family; hence these disciplines are stressed as part of the spiritual path."[3]

We need soulmates like we need earth under our feet and rain to moisten the soil. But what is a soulmate? The word conjures up an image of someone rare and priceless — almost impossible to find. And if we find one on our journey, we tend to hold on for dear life, because we think they come around only once. When we think of a soulmate, we may envision someone who understands us perfectly, loves us with devotion, mirrors our every thought, or "matches" our own soul like a missing mitten. And those kinds of soulmates are nice to find! But they are not the only kind.

A soulmate does not have to be a permanent partner, a lover, a best friend, or a guru — nor does he or she have to be your mirror or your missing piece. A soulmate can be anyone who accompanies you on some portion of your soul's journey through this life and makes that journey richer or sweeter.

All of us have the opportunity to travel with other souls, to form a community of the heart that eases the loneliness of spiritual isolation. Some of us are fortunate to find one or two people in our lives whose souls seem to be shaped like ours. When we connect, we resonate at the deepest levels. We can talk and listen and be understood nearly effortlessly; sometimes no words need pass between us at all. We celebrate the sweet communion we share as well as the piece of ourselves we recognize in each other.

Whether you are blessed with soulmates who settle into the most comfortable room inside you, or with those who walk with you for just a little while, not one of these people crosses your path by chance. Each is a messenger, sent by God, to give you the wisdom, companionship, comfort, or challenge you need for a particular leg of your spiritual journey.

While part of your community lives around you, in your friends and family and church and neighborhood, the most essential part of your community consists of the people who live inside you — those voices and wisdom and love have made themselves at home in the cockles of your soul. Some of your soulmates may have left this earth long ago, yet they live on inside you; their nurturing or wisdom continues to affect the way you think and live today. You may not even have met some of your soulmates: They may be authors or composers or painters who have reached out from paper, instrument, or canvas to teach you profound truths or affirm deeply held convictions.

Consider your experience of community in a new light. Expand your conception of soulmates. Open your eyes and your heart to the wealth of human companionship available to you every moment. Don't send your soul out onto the high wire of life without its safety net.

> *My definition of [soulmates] has changed. When I started thinking about it, I naively thought, Oh, that means there is one person out there for me. And then there was also the misconception that when I found this soul mate, it would be a euphoric experience — no challenges, no triggers, a heaven-on-earth kind of thing. Wrong. I've learned that I have many, many soul mates here, and they come to me at the right time and in the right place. They come to help me when I'm lost, and each comes with different sets of lessons for me.*[4]
>
> — MELODY BEATTIE

•1• Make a list of people who support your growth in any way. Next to each name, write a few words about the type of support the person provides. Over the next year, write a note to each person, acknowledging and expressing your gratitude for the ways they have helped your soul on its journey.

•2• Soulmates come in all ages, shapes, sizes, and colors. Sometimes, the friend who is least like you is the friend you need the most — to challenge your preconceptions and add spice or balance to your life. Ask yourself who, in your orbit of relationships, might fit this description and invite her to lunch.

•3• Rather than running out to create community, realize that you're already part of one. Take a careful look around you — at home, work, school, church, in your neighborhood and professional and civic affiliations — and really *see* the people who are already in your life. What can you do to strengthen your connections with some of them and experience them as your soulmates?

> *We have all known the long loneliness and we have learned that the only solution is love and that love comes with community.*[5]
>
> — DOROTHY DAY

•4• Invite a group of friends to meet over coffee. Ask each to bring one item that particularly reflects her spiritual goals for the year: a budding flower could represent a new beginning; a photograph of still water may symbolize a desire for peace; a wrench could mean . . . well, she brought it, she should know what it means! Make a point of asking one another in the year ahead how your spiritual goals are being fulfilled.

•5• Believe it or not, you have a story to tell. Though it may never be the basis of a best-selling novel, the ongoing story of your life contains ingredients for deepening your relationships. Open up to a friend and you'll soon find him sharing his story with you. The result will be joys increased and sorrows lessened.

•6• Strike up a friendship with someone who's at least twenty years older than you, a person who seems to have aged well emotionally and spiritually. You'll enjoy a new dimension of friendship and learn more about life just by being with him.

> *Find inspiring people. Inspiring people are vitamins for our spirits. They come in all kinds of disguises and descriptions. Inspiring people help us to experience life in a new way. The delight moves us. If you open your heart to being inspired, they will appear.*[6]
>
> — SARK

•7• Some of us suffer from friendship overload — more people in our lives than we have time for. Many of these folks are not close friends but rather acquaintances we have collected over the years. Hard as it may be, take some time to think about which relationships it might be time to let go of and which it might be time to invest in even more.

•8• You may have had a soulmate and lost track of him or her. Even if years and miles separate you, consider writing a letter or picking up the phone. Look into software or World Wide Web sites that list telephone directories all over the country. You might rekindle a friendship that will enrich you both.

•9• Is there someone you were once close to but from whom you have become estranged? If a relationship with a soulmate has been broken through misunderstanding, betrayal, or neglect, consider what part you can play in restoring the relationship. Even if you never again share deeply in each other's journeys, you can honor the person's positive impact on you by offering amends or extending forgiveness.

Faith, like light, should always be simple and unbending; while love, like warmth, should beam forth on every side, and bend to every necessity of our brethren.[7]
— MARTIN LUTHER

•10• Some people are meant to walk with us throughout our whole lives; others are friends for a season. It can be difficult to let go of a relationship that has changed or ended because of physical distance, diverging paths, or changed lifestyles. Take some time to evaluate relationships that have changed. Do something symbolic to say good-bye to the past and thank God for the important role each person played in your life at a special time.

•11• Prayer between friends is one of the greatest gifts you can give each other. Take time when you get together to pray with and for each other. If you can't arrange a personal visit as often as you would like, call each other and pray over the phone. Remember to keep confidences confidential.

•12• Next time you pray, stop for a moment to think about all the other human beings who are praying at the same moment. Reach out with your spirit to consciously connect with praying people throughout the world as you enter into your own prayer.

•**13**• Check out some of the chat rooms on the Internet that are devoted to spiritual topics. You might find some kindred spirits all over the globe.

•**14**• Find a spiritual director, someone who has been living the life of the spirit for many years, someone you admire and trust. If you don't know anyone like this, monasteries can be a great source for finding wise guides.

> *The best mirror is a trusted, old friend.*[8]
> — SEPHARDIC SAYING

•**15**• Who are the five or six people who have had the most influence over your soul's development during your lifetime? Gather photographs of these special folks, or objects that remind you of them, and set up a temporary "shrine of remembrance" in their honor. Each time you pass it, take a moment to thank God for sending each of these people into your life.

•**16**• Think about people you have never met who have had an impact on your spiritual journey. If they are alive, try tracking down an address where you can write to them, thanking them for their contribution to your life. If they are dead, devise a creative way of offering thanks: write a poem or letter you don't mail, place something that reminds you of them in a prominent place in your home, make something with your hands as a tribute to them.

❧

[There is] a man who is quite alone, without a son or brother, yet he works hard to keep gaining more riches, and to whom will he leave it all? And why is he giving up so much now? It is all so pointless and depressing. Two can accomplish more than twice as much as one, for the results can be much better. If one falls, the other pulls him up; but if a man falls when he is alone, he's in trouble. Also, on a cold night, two under the same blanket gain warmth from each other, but how can one be warm alone? And one standing alone can be attacked and defeated, but two can stand back-to-back and conquer; three is even better, for a triple-braided cord is not easily broken.[9]

— KING SOLOMON

•17• If a soulmate of yours has died, mark a day on the calendar to remember him or her each year. On that day, pay tribute in your own way: write to him in your journal, keep a candle burning all day in his honor, visit a place that was special to you both, surround yourself with objects or smells or sounds that remind you of him, and give thanks.

•18• If you are fortunate to have a soulmate who is as close to you as a twin, guard against taking her for granted. Do something in the year ahead to honor her in a new way: commit to pray for her every single day, and do it; take her on a weekend getaway that will create special memories for both of you; mail her a greeting card every month, telling her one way she reflects God to you.

•19• On your next birthday, invite your most valued soulmates to a party in their honor. Write each of them a card, thanking them very specifically for the gifts they have given you through their friendship, and give them each a small, carefully chosen gift that symbolizes to you the nature of their contribution to your life. Share some of your thoughts about each person — including anyone who can't attend — with the rest of the group. Make it a sacred time of gratitude and community.

•**20**• What are the three or four most important qualities you look for in a friend? Over the next twelve months, devote yourself to developing these qualities in yourself. Practice expressing them in all your interactions.

> *The beauty of [a friend] is only a taste of what God is. It should be seen as an image of God and an enticement towards him. If the two try to spend their lives trying to look at each other only, they will never be open to the absolute fullness in God of which this friend is only a taste.*[10]
>
> — Paul Hinnebusch

•8•

SOUL WORKOUT

Laziness and cowardice are two of the greatest enemies of the spiritual life.[1]
— Thomas Merton

No matter how motivated we may be to nurture our spiritual life, we all have a lazy bone in our soul. It's just part of being human and, too often, deceived by the allure and urgency of whatever activity or obligation is pressing on us at the moment.

Albert Schweitzer called our propensity to get caught up in the trivial "a sleeping sickness of the soul. Its most dangerous aspect is that one is unaware of its coming. That is why you have to be careful. As soon as you notice the slightest sign of indifference, the moment you become aware of the loss of a certain seriousness, of longing, of enthusiasm and zest, take it as a warning. You should realize that your soul suffers if you live superficially."[2]

Living attentively to the needs and potential of the soul requires effort. Just as the body does not become fit while lounging on the couch, the soul does not become strong and resilient without exercise. What do you do to keep your body in shape? And what are the results? Chances are, unless you were born with unusual genes, your muscles and organs are about as fit as you make them through diet and exercise. The same is true for the soul: No one is born with a soul that doesn't need lifelong attention and exercise in order to stay fit.

Spiritual exercise can include practicing some of the "classic" spiritual disciplines identified by religious practitioners throughout the ages: prayer, meditation, fasting, reading inspirational texts, silence, worship, service, giving. It can also involve less-structured activities like some of the vitamins suggested in other chapters. Whatever exercise you choose, spiritual health requires consistency and dedication — regular workouts.

Someone has said that "yearning for God is not safe if you want to stay as you are."[3] Yearning for just about anything isn't safe if we don't want to do the work it usually takes to achieve our goals. Waking up your soul by taking the vitamins in this book will kindle a yearning in you that can't be ignored. Once the vitamins start to flow in, your hunger for spiritual sustenance will continue to grow. What will you do to feed it? How will you exercise your new spiritual muscles?

Your soul's lazy bone might try to pull you down on the spiritual sofa for a little more lounging around than is good for you — so pay attention. Listen to your soul just as you listen to your body. What does it need today? What does it need to stay healthy over the long term?

The great thing about spiritual exercise is that it doesn't leave you sore and limping; it invigorates you and reconnects you to everything that is most important in life.

> *A spiritual life without discipline is impossible. . . . The practice of a spiritual discipline makes us more sensitive to the small, gentle voice of God.*[4]
>
> — HENRI NOUWEN

•1• Draw a line down the center of a piece of paper and label the two columns "Laziness" and "Fear." Jot down the thoughts that come to mind about how these two issues interfere with working on your spiritual life. Add to the list throughout the week as more insights come to you.

•2• Exercising your soul takes dedication and determination. It costs you something. But failing to do so costs you even more. Spend ten minutes thinking about everything you stand to lose if you fail to take your spiritual life seriously — things like a deep sense of peace and joy, guidance about important decisions, the knowledge that your life has meaning, confidence that God is in charge no matter what. Make your own list and let it motivate you when you are tempted to give up or cut corners.

•3• Francois Fenelon says, "There is only one way to love God: to take not a single step without him, and to follow with a brave heart wherever he leads."[5] What might the next forty-eight hours of your life look like if you took Fenelon's words to heart?

> *In everything remember your end, and remember that time lost cannot be called back again. Without labor and diligence you will never get virtue. If you begin to be negligent, you begin to be feeble and weak. But if you apply yourself with fervor, you will find great help from God.*[6]
>
> — THOMAS À KEMPIS

•4• If "working out" spiritually isn't a priority for you, make a list of all the reasons why. What does this list reveal about yourself and your beliefs?

•5• When you begin to practice discipline in any area of your life, it usually feels unpleasant and burdensome. To counteract this reality, try carrying out your acts of discipline with what Edward Hays calls a "generous heart."[7] Give each exercise your full attention and fill your efforts with all the love and gratitude you can muster. You may find that what at first feels like drudgery becomes a joyful song of the soul.

•6• If you are a regular churchgoer, pick a Sunday to attend a church where you don't know anyone. Go alone, and solely for the purpose of worship. Keep your mind focused on God throughout the service; bring a heightened consciousness to the hymns, readings, sermon, Eucharist, etc. Ask God to touch your soul with the joy of his presence.

> *Spiritual sloth happens when the pleasure is removed from the spiritual life. Such souls become weary with spiritual exercises because they do not yield any consolation, and thus, they abandon them. They begin to lose interest in God for they measure God by themselves and not themselves by God.*[8]
>
> — St. John of the Cross

•7• How much silence do you allow in your daily life? How can you use silence as a spiritual discipline — a way to move from the dead end of self-focus to the consolation of God-focus? Try it this week.

•8• Buy one of the many books of daily inspirational readings available at your local bookstore. Get up ten minutes early every day this week and review the day's reading. Choose a line to meditate on throughout the hours ahead. Write it down and put it in your pocket or planner.

•9• The biblical book of Proverbs is packed with timeless wisdom you can use every day. Find it in a Bible, or buy a copy of Eugene Peterson's modern translation, simply called *Proverbs*, and read one verse each morning before you start your day. At the end of the day, reflect on how the wisdom came to you when you needed it — or on how you wish you'd heeded it!

> *The classical Disciplines of the spiritual life call us to move beyond surface living into the depths. They invite us to explore the inner caverns of the spiritual realm. They urge us to be the answer to a hollow world.*[9]
>
> — RICHARD J. FOSTER

•10• Make mealtime sacred by offering a regular prayer of thanksgiving. Use your own words to express your gratitude or try this traditional Jewish grace:

Blessed are You, O Lord our God,
King of the universe
who feeds the whole world with
Your goodness, grace, kindness and mercy.
You give food to all flesh,
for Your mercy endures forever.
Through Your great goodness, we have never lacked food:
may it never fail us,
for the sake of Your great Name,
for You nourish and sustain all beings,
and do good to all,
and provide food for all Your creatures
whom You have created.
Blessed are You, O Lord, who give food to all.[10]

•11• For five minutes, close your eyes and repeat a word or phrase that helps you tune into your soul. One that has been used by millions since the sixth century is the Jesus Prayer: "Lord Jesus Christ, Son of God, have mercy on me, a sinner." Use it or come up with a short prayer of your own.

•12• Choose a habit you would like to cultivate and dedicate the next month to forming it. Here are a few ideas: Tell your children you love them as you tuck them into bed each night; set aside ten minutes a day for spiritual reading; compliment your spouse on something he does well; use family mealtimes to talk about all that went right in your day; accept the compliments that come your way.

•13• Find a regular way to give your time unselfishly: Spend an evening playing games with your kids when you'd rather work or relax; make a date with your spouse that's focused on making her feel special; volunteer at a local social agency. Do it all in the spirit of letting go of your own self-centeredness.

A fasting attitude multiplies the enrichment while it minimizes the consumption. And it gives birth to freedom. We can learn the freedom of getting along with less clothing, less heat, less sound to fill our silences, less objects to fill our spaces, less diversions to fill our time. The little, when given a chance to blossom and express all its own proper reality, can with its beauty fill to overflowing all our capacities. As we grow in gratitude and appreciation we need less and less of creation; we are freer and freer to find in ourselves and in the expansive little we already have, all that we want and need.[11]

— M. Basil Pennington

•14• Choose a month this year to cultivate a "fasting attitude." During each week of the month, focus on one area of your life — your possessions, your diversions, your appetites — and consciously diminish your consumption. Keep a daily or weekly journal of the thoughts, feelings, and experiences this exercise brings up for you.

•15• One day this week eat nothing after noontime; drink only water. Notice how many times your thoughts turn toward satisfying your appetite or anxiety with food or drink. Each time your thoughts move in this direction, stop and say a prayer, thanking God for the ways your needs are met each day.

•16• Choose a charity whose cause you support and make a commitment to give a regular cash gift each month for a year.

•17• Take your favorite TV, sports, or fun night and use the time to serve others. Clean out your closets and make a donation to the Salvation Army, offer to answer phones for a crisis hotline, visit with someone in a nursing home, call someone you know who is lonely or struggling.

> *I always give much away and so gather happiness instead of pleasure.*[12]
>
> — RACHEL VARNHAGEN

•18• In our materialistic culture it's all too easy to stuff ourselves full of *things,* which can stunt our souls and impoverish our hearts. To make sure your possessions aren't possessing you, give something you cherish to someone you cherish — a sacrificial gift that will enrich both your lives.

•19• Giving to the less fortunate can be a

great way to stretch your soul and enlarge your vision of life. Paradoxically, generosity can actually increase your peace and lessen your anxiety about your financial situation. Instead of money having power over you, generosity gives you power over money. Try looking over your checkbook register for the past year to see what's happening to all those greenbacks, and decide how you could refocus your spending in order to give more to others.

•20• Rosh Hashanah marks the beginning of the Jewish New Year. Also known as the Day of Remembrance, it begins a ten-day period of spiritual self-examination known as the Ten Days of Awe. Set aside several days at the start of each year to mark your own days of awe.

> *Awake, ye sleepers from your sleep . . . and ponder over your deeds; remember your Creator and go back to Him in penitence. Be not of those who miss realities in their pursuit of shadows and waste their years in seeking after vain things which cannot profit or deliver. Look well to your souls and consider your acts; forsake each of you his wrong ways and improper thoughts and return to God so that He may have mercy on you.*[13]
>
> — Moses Maimonides

•9•

LIGHTENING YOUR SOUL

Being too serious is habit-forming.[1]
— KAREN CASEY

While some treasures can be mined only through patient, laborious excavation, others are all around you for the taking. Nurturing your spiritual life is a lifelong task to be taken seriously, but you've missed the point if you make it all work and no play. When you take your soul vitamins faithfully, you'll be more aware of what's important in life, more present to other people, and more serene as you feed your soul what it craves. But if you're not also more joyful, more excited about life, and more confident that God is lovingly involved in the universe, then you're missing a vital nutrient.

A healthy soul is a happy soul. Laughter comes more easily to someone whose spirit is being nurtured and who, as a result, has a realistic perspective on life. Realistic people are not Pollyannas who refuse to look upon the inevitable suffering that living on this planet entails, but neither do they allow that suffering to steal their gratitude and joy over the many earthly and heavenly realities worth celebrating. No one says it better than the late Dutch priest Henri Nouwen: "Joyful persons do not necessarily make jokes, laugh, or even smile. They are not people with an optimistic outlook on life who always relativize the seriousness of a moment or an event. No, joyful persons see with open eyes the hard reality of human existence and at the same time are not imprisoned by it. They suffer with those who suffer, yet they do not hold on to suffering; they point beyond it to an everlasting peace."[2]

No matter what you're facing today — whether it be the fears and uncertainties of transition, the pesky irritations of the day-to-day, the thrill of new love or opportunity, or the heartache of loss — taking your joy vitamins is essential. Someone has said, "The opposite of joy is not sorrow. It is unbelief."[3] If we do not believe in the essential goodness of God, in the enormous potential of the human spirit, and in the ultimate victory of light over darkness, then celebration in the midst of life's harsh realities is laughable — and even the laughs we do experience when life is "good" ring hollow.

When you look into your soul, do you see

darkness or light? Sorrow or joy? If you're honest, you'll recognize both. And as you grow spiritually, you'll embrace both. You won't be shrouded in gloom or transported by superficial frivolity. You will drink your cup of sorrow, but it won't be lethal to your soul. You won't have to escape suffering by pretending it's not as bad as it is; neither will you be deceived by its harshness: Life is still a gift, God is still in charge. There is cause for celebration.

Writer and speaker Luci Swindoll gives us a wake-up call: "Each of us is surrounded by opportunities to become excited and involved in activities at hand. But we're waiting for the other shoe to drop. We're wanting things to get better, to lighten up, to go away. We're waiting for a ship to come in that never went out."[4] Don't make the mistake of waiting to *live*. This is it. This is your precious time on earth.

A wise king once said:

There is a time for everything,
and a season for every activity under heaven:
a time to be born and a time to die,
a time to plant and a time to uproot,
a time to kill and a time to heal,
a time to tear down and a time to build,
a time to weep and a time to laugh,

a time to mourn and a time to dance,
a time to scatter stones and a time to gather them,
a time to embrace and a time to refrain,
a time to search and a time to give up,
a time to keep and a time to throw away,
a time to tear and a time to mend,
a time to be silent and a time to speak,
a time to love and a time to hate,
a time for war and a time for peace.[5]

Embrace the whole ball of wax. Don't leave out a single ingredient. But when you're mourning, don't forget that life is also for dancing. When your dreams are being torn apart, don't forget that God also gives new dreams. And when you're weeping, don't forget that "weeping may last for the night, but a shout of joy comes in the morning."[6]

Our poor, splendid souls! How they fight for food! They have forgotten how to celebrate. Our hurried, stressful, busy lives are unquestionably the most dangerous enemy of celebrating life itself. Somehow, we must learn how to achieve momentary slow-downs, and request from God a heightened awareness of the conception that life is a happy thing, a festival to be enjoyed rather than a drudgery to be endured.[7]

— LUCI SWINDOLL

•**1**• Buy one of the many attractive blank books available at your local bookstore and designate it your "Life Affirmations" book. During the year ahead, fill it with positive thoughts, quotes, funny stories, jokes, memories, hopes — anything that affirms that life is a festival to be enjoyed. Then when you have a bad day or a grumpy attitude, you'll have some reminders at your fingertips of why you still have cause for celebration.

•**2**• The Apostle Paul offers a good prescription for negativity: "Whatever is true, whatever is noble, whatever is right, whatever is pure, whatever is lovely, whatever is admirable — if anything is excellent or praiseworthy — think about such things."[8] Next time you find yourself dwelling on what's wrong in life, make a choice to shift your focus.

•3• If you are not in the habit of laughing a lot, you'd better not wait until something strikes you as funny. Many of us adults have to relearn how to giggle and laugh, and it starts with a desire. If you want to laugh more, make a decision to do it. Then cut loose!

> *No matter how much pain, abuse, or injustice we may suffer or cause others to suffer, a certain delightfulness remains within us that can never be destroyed. And somehow, at some point in every situation, there is always an invitation to join the play.*[9]
>
> — GERALD MAY

•4• Try capping your day with a chuckle by following Robert Fulghum's example: "To end the day, I do a funny thing before I go to sleep. I read something humorous in bed. Joke books, cartoon books — I'll read anything to help me go to bed with a laugh in my mind. This annoys my wife, because I get to laughing and shaking the bed, and then I have to read her the story or joke."[10]

•5• Buy a copy of *Inspiration Sandwich* or

Living Juicy by writer and artist Sark. If you don't get more excited and delighted about life by reading her prose, check your pulse.

•6• Take a giggle break with A. A. Milne's *Winnie-the-Pooh* or *The House at Pooh Corner.* The antics of Winnie, Piglet, Tigger, and Eeyore are always good for a chuckle.

> *Laughter, like a drenching rain, settles the dust, cleans and brightens the world around us, and changes our whole perspective.*[11]
>
> — JAN PISHOK

•7• In his book *Anatomy of an Illness*, Norman Cousins makes a convincing case for the power of humor to heal physical maladies. (King Solomon prescribed it centuries before when he said: "A cheerful heart is good medicine, but a crushed spirit dries up the bones.") Part of Cousins's personal therapy involved watching one funny movie after another. Find some movies that suit your unique sense of humor and make a night of it. Here are some possibilities to check out at your local video store:

Father of the Bride
Abbott and Costello Meet the Invisible Man

The Cocoanuts
The Philadelphia Story
What About Bob?
Sister Act
Uncle Buck
Planes, Trains, and Automobiles
City Slickers
Junior
National Lampoon's Christmas Vacation
Crimes and Misdemeanors
Home Alone

•8• A little silliness can sometimes lighten your load. Designate a dresser drawer as your "fun drawer," filling it with things you enjoy: colorful mugs, hand puppets, humorous greeting cards, stuffed animals that make you smile, bubbles or bubble bath, funny books, games, pictures of your favorite people — whatever strikes your fancy. Then, whenever the mood or need hits, send the cards, fill a mug with some delicious brew, or blow bubbles in your bubble bath. (The latter is even more fun if you have a small child to play with.)

•9• Think about something you would have loved to do as a kid but never got the chance. Then do it. Who's stopping you from climbing on a horse and riding into the sunset? Or wearing your very own Mickey Mouse ears while you scream on the Matterhorn at Disneyland? Or sledding down the steepest hill in the neighborhood after the next winter storm? Go for it.

> *All the days of the oppressed are wretched, but the cheerful heart has a continual feast.*[12]
>
> — KING SOLOMON

•10• Laughter is not intended to be merely a Band-Aid to conceal misery. If you're unhappy about something, spend at least twenty minutes thinking about how you can move from the problem into a solution. Nothing creates positive energy more than positive action. Don't be one of the people Richard Foster says are "looking for some kind of heavenly transfusion that will bypass the misery of their daily lives and give them joy. God's desire is not to bypass the misery but to transform it."[13]

•11• Take advantage of opportunities to attend festivals of celebration in your community. Wherever large numbers of people are gathered to have fun, join them!

•12• Next time you're feeling glum, visit a

shop that carries an array of greeting cards and spend some time reading the funny ones. Don't be afraid to laugh out loud; it will give other card shoppers permission to do the same thing!

> *The laughter of a child is unprogrammed, genuine, and brand new. All the forms and the techniques of humor are responded to. A sixty-year-old knows what he is supposed to laugh at and knows all the taboos, but a child is a fresh slate.*[14]
>
> — John Bailey

•13• Kids can be our best teachers of how to have fun, as well as a great source of entertainment. After all, most of them aren't afraid to be downright goofy! Tell your kids and their friends that you'll supply the props if they'll provide the entertainment, and ask them to put on an original play for family and friends. Not only will you be amazed at their creativity, but you'll enjoy a lot of laughs.

•14• Watch cartoons or fun videos with some youngsters and let their bubbling, unself-conscious laughter feed your soul. Have fun together.

•15• Make silly faces at a baby. If you're in a bad mood, you won't stay that way when she smiles back.

•16• If you have a good toy store in your town, give yourself thirty minutes to explore every aisle. Make sure to play with anything you can get your hands on. Take a couple of your adult friends with you; you'll be surprised at how much you'll laugh together.

> *A hearty laugh feels great! At that magical moment of laughter, we feel relaxed, hopeful, open, and forgiving. We no longer feel anxious, hostile, depressed, or alone.*[15]
>
> — PATTY WOOTEN, R.N.

•17• Who makes you laugh? Make sure to spend regular time with this person. Also fill your life with people who have a good sense of humor and a positive attitude. Negativity is every bit as contagious as laughter, and you don't want to catch it — or spread it.

•18• Laughter is highly contagious. If you're *really* brave (and nutty), try this tried-and-true exercise recommended by Dr. Raymond A. Moody, Jr., an expert on the healing power of humor: Form a human chain, with the head of each person lying on the abdomen of someone else. Designate one person to start laughing (as if you could stop it from happening!) and experience the belly laugh "wave" as it travels down the chain. In no time you'll have a mini-epidemic of hilarity on your hands.[16]

•19• One of King Solomon's wise proverbs states: "A happy heart makes the face cheerful."[17] That's easy to understand. But another one says: "A cheerful look brings joy to the heart."[18] Next time you think the egg has to come before the chicken, that you can't smile or laugh until you feel happy, try reversing your assumptions. Put a smile on your face, or force yourself to chuckle. If you do it in front of the mirror, you may find that your halfhearted effort will turn into a genuinely fun moment.

•20• Make a list of the things that cause you to put joy and celebration on hold. Try finishing this sentence: "I'll be happy when . . ." Or this one: "I would feel better if only he/she would . . ." Then take yourself to task. Who is responsible for your attitude and your happiness?

I believe that I know and share the many sorrows and sad circumstances that a human being can experience, but I do not cling to them, I do not prolong such moments of agony. They pass through me, like life itself, as a broad, eternal stream, they become part of that stream, and life continues. And as a result all my strength is preserved, does not become tagged on to futile sorrow.[19]

— ETTY HILLESUM

•10•

YOUR SOUL IN ACTION

We do not adequately honor God unless we do all we can to encourage and bring out the goodness and beauty of our fellowmen.[1]

— PAUL HINNEBUSCH

"Why am I here?" Paying attention to your soul ultimately prompts the question. Are you growing your soul just so you'll feel better? Or is there a bigger reason?

Too many people consider soul work to be primarily interior and valuable only to the person doing the work. The most important reason to attend to our souls, however, is that spiritual health and vitality determines the quality of our contribution to our world. What good is a healthy soul hidden away on a mountaintop or "purified" to the point of divorce from reality?

Alan Jones's words bite with the truth that "there are those who think that they love God because they don't love anyone else."[2] But God is not impressed with antiseptic spirituality. Spiritual wholeness is not an end in itself; it is a means to participate fully in a world that is spiritually hungry. A healthy soul cannot help but love.

Dr. Avram Davis defines spiritual enlightenment not as transcendence but as engagement: A whole soul "lives fully in the world, savoring it, loving it, engaging *passionately* with it. Our task is not to remove our attachments to the world but to strengthen them."[3] Thomas Moore agrees: "The aim of soul work is not adjustment to accepted norms or to an image of the statistically healthy individual. Rather, the goal is a richly elaborated life, connected to society and nature, woven into the culture of family, nation, and globe. The idea is not to be superficially adjusted, but to be profoundly connected to brothers and sisters in all the many communities that claim our hearts."[4]

But who are your brothers and sisters? What is the world in which you are called to live fully? Is it the homeless at your local soup kitchen? The needy in the ghettos of Calcutta? The broken in the county detox center? Yes, the world is all of these, and it calls for our loving engagement. But the world you're here to participate in starts much closer to home. Loving the world begins with being present to your own child, listening tenderly to your spouse, forgiving your mother's foibles. It means making eye contact and real conversation with your neighbor before punching the button on your garage door and disappearing into your castle. It means consciously looking for ways to be generous of spirit, to give your world some of the richness growing inside you.

And what about that most daunting directive of all: "Love your enemies, do good to those who hate you"?[5] That's a tough pill to swallow, partly because it has been misunderstood and misused to compel hurt people to continue to be abused by others.But when properly understood as a divine strategic weapon to bring an evil person to his knees, doing good can be the ultimate act of love. Consider the words of Dr. Dan Allender, who has spent years helping sexual abuse victims deal with their perpetrators' treachery: "Love is not weak, fear-based compliance. Love is not an absence of anger. Love also does not minimize or forget past harm. Love is not pious other-centeredness that is devoid of pleasure for the giver. Love that is so spiritualized that it reflects an absence of humanness is neither spiritual nor human. Love is essentially a movement of grace to embrace those who have sinned against us. Love can be defined as *the free gift that vol-*

untarily cancels the debt in order to free the debtor to become what he might be if he experiences the joy of restoration."[6]

Love is a multifaceted, complex, powerful gift from God that will change the world when we use it well. It is far more than a sugary emotion, a vague sensation of goodwill, or even a fierce devotion that makes promises of ultimate sacrifice. Love without action is dead. And a life spent in devotion to anything but love will never fulfill its destiny. Robert Hugh Benson says it succinctly: "It is only the souls that do not love that go empty in this world."[7]

So why are *you* here? Spend some serious time with the question. Then put your whole soul into living the answer.

> *You are here in order to enable the world to live more amply, with greater vision, with a finer spirit of hope and achievement. You are here to enrich the world, and you impoverish yourself if you forget the errand.*[8]
>
> — Woodrow Wilson

•1• Spend some time reflecting on the ways in which your presence on earth enriches the world. Start at home, then consider your circle of friends, your community, your country, your planet. Be as specific as you can, thanking God for the personal qualities and resources he's given you that enable you to enrich others. Then consider additional ways in which you might enable the world to live more amply. Even something as small as recycling your household waste or giving canned goods to a local homeless shelter can make a difference.

•2• Become an answer to someone else's prayer. Visit a sick relative or friend, call someone and encourage them, mow a neighbor's yard, give your spouse a back rub, write a check for a local charity, compliment a coworker, volunteer at a shelter for the homeless. Lift your spirits by lifting someone else's load.

•3• Think of something you do particularly well: Perhaps it's accounting, gardening, cooking, organizing, singing, plumbing, listening. Turn your unique talent into a service during the year ahead. Offer to help a friend with her tax return; bake a pie for a different neighbor each month; volunteer to drive senior citizens to appointments and really listen to them en route.

The birth of righteousness and love in this stern world is always a virgin birth. It is never men nor the nations of men nor all the power and wisdom of men that bring it forth but always God.[9]

— Frederick Buechner

•**4**• Practice acknowledging that you, an imperfect human being, will always run out of patience, tolerance, and compassion unless you are filled with the character of the only One who loves perfectly. Next time you are with someone who is difficult for you to love, pull inside yourself for a moment and ask God to fill you with his perfect love. Repeat this exercise of humility and surrender as many times as you need to until you see the evidence of his love in your attitude and behavior.

•**5**• Make a list of qualities you would like to develop to a higher degree in your life — things like courage, honesty, compassion, generosity, humility, faithfulness. Ask for guidance in deciding which of these to focus on right now, then ask God for grace to grow this trait. Get ready for an adventure. Plenty of opportunities to exercise your virtue of choice will be heading your way!

•6• If you have a parent or grandparent who is getting on in years, commit regular time to interview them about their life. Come up with some great questions, tape-record or videotape your loved one, honor them by giving them a listening ear and a platform to share who they are and what life has taught them. Consider writing or recording their biography for everyone in the family to learn from and enjoy.

> *"You shall love your neighbor as yourself." This is a strange command, really. How can we be commanded to love? We can be asked, cajoled — but ordered? What if your neighbor is a fiend, a horror? We can answer this only with the admonition to look deeper. Every soul is a fragment of the Infinite. Should we not love and feel compassion for such a pure thing that has become lost amid the shells of illusion?*[10]
>
> — AVRAM DAVIS

•7• This week think about one person who really rubs you the wrong way. Pray each day for that person. (No fair asking God to change *him* so he'll stop irritating *you.*) Just ask a simple blessing on him and see what happens.

•**8**• Spend some time reflecting on the words of Jesus' apostle John: "Anyone who claims to be in the light but hates his brother is still in the darkness."[11] Is there anyone you hate? Are you willing to move into the light? How can you begin?

•**9**• As an act of faith and obedience to the divine command to love, do something kind for someone you think doesn't "deserve" your goodwill. Bake some bread for some unfriendly neighbors and present it with a warm smile; spend time with a crotchety relative and *really* listen — beneath her words — to her legitimate human needs; commit yourself to serving people you consider the "undesirables" in your community in a specific way.

•**10**• Read Matthew 23:1–33 and John 8:1–11 in the New Testament and take an honest look at yourself. In what ways do you harbor the attitude of a Pharisee? Of whom do you stand in judgment? Ask God what concrete gesture of humility and genuine love you could make to that person in the year ahead; then commit to doing it.

To love at all is to be vulnerable. Love anything, and your heart will certainly be wrung and possibly be broken. If you want to make sure of keeping it intact, you must give your heart to no one, not even to an animal. Wrap it carefully round with hobbies and little luxuries; avoid all entanglements; lock it up safe in the casket or coffin of your selfishness. But in that casket — safe, dark, motionless, airless — it will change. It will not be broken; it will become unbreakable, impenetrable, irredeemable.[12]

— C. S. Lewis

•11• Is there anything you feel called to do but have resisted? Perhaps you could make a meaningful contribution by serving at a local hospice, battered women's shelter, or prison. Perhaps you'd be a good Sunday-school teacher, Big Brother or Big Sister, child advocate in your county court system, or volunteer at your local animal shelter. What fear or selfishness is stopping you? Bite the bullet and choose one avenue of involvement to commit to for six months. At the end of that time, reevaluate your fears and selfish concerns and ask God how you should proceed with your commitment or redirect it.

•**12**• Befriend an elderly widow in your neighborhood and find out how you can help her with household chores throughout the year. Get your whole family involved. Become someone she can count on to shovel snow, rake leaves, make minor repairs, carry in groceries, wash windows, etc. Be willing to be inconvenienced for the sake of showing love.

•**13**• During the Christmas holidays, "adopt" a needy family and provide some gifts for their children and food for their table. Better yet, offer to take the children gift shopping, help the family put up holiday decorations, or invite them to Christmas dinner. Make actively caring for others a focal point for your family every Christmas.

> *If I speak with human eloquence and angelic ecstasy but don't love, I'm nothing but the creaking of a rusty gate. If I speak God's Word with power, revealing all his mysteries and making everything plain as day, and if I have faith that says to a mountain, "Jump," and it jumps, but I don't love, I'm nothing. If I give everything I own to the poor and even go to the stake to be burned as a martyr, but I don't love, I've gotten nowhere. So, no matter what I say, what I believe, and what I do, I'm bankrupt without love.*[13]
>
> — THE APOSTLE PAUL

•14• For the next seven days, make a point of finding a way to tell someone you care about him without using words. Be creative!

•15• Sometimes we make the mistake of loving people in the ways *we* want to be loved instead of in the ways that would mean the most to them. Consider the needs of some of the most important people in your life. What do you think they most want from you? Come up with a few custom-made ways to show your love for them in the month ahead.

•16• When's the last time someone complimented you? Unfortunately, encouragement can be as rare as butterflies in a blizzard. Make it a practice to praise one person every day. Forming this habit may not change the whole world, but it may have an impact in ways you can't calculate.

•**17**• Alan Paton said, "Both Jesus and his great disciple [Paul] accepted the wound in the creation, and having accepted it, devoted their lives to the healing of it. *That* is the creative act, not to ask who dealt this wound to the creation, not to accuse God of having dealt it, but to make of one's life an instrument of God's peace. This act is doubly creative, in that it transforms both giver and receiver."[14] Consider how much time and energy you expend complaining about a person or situation beyond your control. Then consider some ways in which you can operate as an instrument of God's peace instead. This may take some long and creative thinking, but the results will transform you as well as the situation.

Each day you are faced with opportunities to help others, to forgive them, to have compassion for them, to be tolerant of them. Do you seize these opportunities, or do you let them slip by? Though seemingly inconsequential, these everyday decisions have direct impact on the state of your soul, for you nurture your soul by giving of yourself to others in a loving way. And each time you choose to help others, your soul grows and flourishes.[15]

— JOHN GRAY, PH.D.

•18• Set aside time to think about the first day of your life on earth: the day you were born. Everything was predetermined — the color of your skin, your sex, your temperament, the texture of your hair. The most basic things about you were already in place, given as a gift. Think about it. Cherish the gift. Praise the Giver.

•19• Think about another important day in your life: your last day on earth. Okay, you'd rather not. But do it anyway, for at least thirty minutes. What would you want friends and family to say at your funeral? What will they remember most? Do you see any burned bridges? Does anyone hold a grudge that will trail you to the grave? If you're not happy about what you envision, do something about it. Today is not too early to begin.

•20• It has been said that no one, at the end of his life, wishes he had spent more time at the office. He probably doesn't kick himself for not watching more TV or keeping a cleaner house either. Spend some time now, while you can, thinking about what's most important to you. When you're on your deathbed, how will you wish you had spent your time? Do whatever you have to do to make your lifestyle line up with your most deeply felt priorities.

He has achieved success who has lived well, laughed often, and loved much; who has gained the respect of intelligent men and the love of little children; who has filled his niche and accomplished his task; who has left the world better than he found it, whether by an improved poppy, a perfect poem, or a rescued soul; who has never lacked appreciation of earth's beauty or failed to express it; who has always looked for the best in others and given the best he had; whose life was an inspiration; whose memory a benediction.[16]

— ANONYMOUS

•AFTERWORD•

We hope you have swallowed some of our vitamins and experienced the benefits. When you start giving your soul what it craves, your appetite only increases. We encourage you to continue to use this book in the months and years ahead whenever you need a reminder of how to nurture your deepest self. Remember your need for solitude and reflection, rest and healing, prayer and discipline, spiritual companions, wonder, laughter, and solid soul food. Doing so will strengthen your resolve to continue nurturing your soul even during times when the demands of life intensify.

Most of all, remember the reason you're nurturing your soul in the first place. It will never be an end in itself. Ponder the words of Frederick Buechner: "We were created in the image of God, but something has gone awry. Like a mirror with a crack down the middle, we give back an image that is badly distorted. We were created to serve God and each other in love, but each of us chooses instead to serve himself as God, and this means wrenching ourselves out of the kind of relationship with God and men that we were made for. Like Adam, we have all lost

Paradise; and yet we carry Paradise around inside of us in the form of a longing for, almost a memory of, a blessedness that is no more, or the dream of a blessedness that may someday be again. In other words, the self that each of us has to live with day in and day out under the most intimate circumstances possible is not entirely the self that we would have chosen to be tied to on such a long-term basis. If the tiger who thinks he is a goat could really be a goat, then he would not have this problem. But fortunately, or unfortunately, there is still enough of the tiger in us to make us discontented with our goathood. We eat grass, but it never really fills us. We bleat well enough, but deep down there is the suspicion that we were really made for roaring."[1]

Don't be satisfied with grass when you need meat to nourish your soul. If you pay close attention to your spiritual nature, you will soon find yourself reflecting the memory and hope of Paradise to a world that yearns to be filled.

•NOTES•

Introduction • Soul Hunger

[1]As quoted in Armand Eisen, ed., *The Spiritual Life*, p. 310.

1• The Care & Feeding of Your Soul

[1]As quoted in Armand Eisen, ed., *The Spiritual Life*, p. 212.

[2]Richard J. Foster, *Celebration of Discipline*, p. 2.

[3]Eugene H. Peterson, *The Message*, Luke 9:25.

[4]As quoted in Phil Cousineau, ed., *Soul, An Archaeology*, p. 142.

[5]As quoted in Luci Shaw, *Water My Soul*, to be published by Zondervan in 1997, Chapter 4.

[6]As quoted in Cousineau, *Soul, An Archaeology*, p. 41.

[7]Annie Dillard, *The Writing Life*, pp. 32–33.

[8]Gregory Post and Charles Turner, *The Feast*, p. 71.

[9]Harry Emerson Fosdick as quoted in Eisen, *The Spiritual Life*, p.92.

[10]*The Holy Bible*, King James Version, Genesis 2:7.

[11]As quoted in Joni Eareckson Tada, *Heaven: Your Real Home*, p.194.

2 • A Touch of Wonder

[1]As quoted in Armand Eisen, ed., *On Being Christian*, p. 251.
[2]As quoted in Phil Cousineau, ed., *Soul, An Archaeology*, p. 184.
[3]As quoted in Cousineau, *Soul, An Archaeology*, p. 188.
[4]Macrina Wiederkehr, O.S.B., *A Tree Full of Angels*, pp. xiii, 28.
[5]Desmond Tutu, *An African Prayer Book*, p. 7.
[6]As quoted in Armand Eisen, ed., *The Spiritual Life*, p. 140.

3 • Taking a Spiritual Vacation

[1]*The New International Version Holy Bible*, Psalm 55:6.
[2]Frederick Buechner, *The Magnificent Defeat*, p. 48.
[3]Judith Couchman, *Shaping a Woman's Soul*, pp. 18–19.
[4]As quoted in Richard J. Foster and James Bryan Smith, *Devotional Classics*, pp. 95–96.
[5]As quoted in Richard Carlson and Benjamin Shield, eds., *Handbook for the Soul*, p. 189.
[6]M. Basil Pennington, O.C.S.O., *A Place Apart*, pp. 31–32.
[7]Richard J. Foster, *Prayer*, pp. 95–96.
[8]*New American Standard Bible*, Matthew 11:28–30.

[9]Eugene H. Peterson, *The Message*, Matthew 5:3–10.
[10]Pennington, *A Place Apart*, pp. 30, 31.

4 • Healing Your Soul

[1]As quoted in Armand Eisen, ed., *The Spiritual Life*, p. 65.
[2]Phil Cousineau, ed., *Soul, An Archaeology*, p. 88.
[3]Sark, *Inspiration Sandwich*, pp. 67–68.
[4]*Alcoholics Anonymous*, p. 64.
[5]*The Living Bible*, Job 10:1–4.
[6]Dan B. Allender, *The Wounded Heart*, p. 176.
[7]St. Augustine, *The Confessions of St. Augustine*, Book 1, Chapter 5.
[8]Henri Nouwen, *Seeds of Hope*, p. 35.
[9]*The New International Version Bible*, Psalm 34:18.
[10]As quoted in Luci Shaw, *Water My Soul*, to be published by Zondervan in 1997, Chapter 4.
[11]As quoted in Mary Ellen Ashcroft and Holly Bridges Elliot, *Bearing Our Sorrows*, p. 41.
[12]Ibid, p. 12.

5 • Soul Food

[1]As quoted in John K. Terres, *Things Precious and Wild*, p. 208.
[2]Thomas Merton, *Thoughts in Solitude*, pp. 62–63.

[3]Annie Dillard, *The Writing Life*, p. 33.
[4]Stephanie Merritt, *Mind, Music and Imagery*, p. 11.
[5]Merritt, *Mind, Music and Imagery*, p. 125.
[6]Helen L. Bonny and Louis M. Savary, *Music & Your Mind*, p. 17.
[7]Irving Stone, *Depths of Glory*, p. 55.
[8]As quoted in Terres, *Things Precious and Wild*, p. 27.
[9]Eugene Peterson, untitled manuscript to be published by Zondervan in 1997.
[10]As quoted in Armand Eisen, ed., *The Spiritual Life*, p. 26.
[11]As quoted in Terres, *Things Precious and Wild*, p. 117.

6 • SOUL TALK

[1]As quoted in Phil Cousineau, ed., *Soul, An Archaeology*, p. 141.
[2]Eugene H. Peterson, *The Message*, Psalm 8:3–8.
[3]As quoted in Mary Ellen Ashcroft and Holly Bridges Elliott, *Bearing Our Sorrows*, p. 66.
[4]As quoted in Armand Eisen, ed., *On Being Christian*, p. 139.
[5]Rebecca Manley Pippert, *Hope Has Its Reasons*, p. 91.
[6]As quoted in Eisen, *On Being Christian*, p. 307.
[7]Oswald Chambers, *If You Will Ask*, p. 10.

[8]Richard J. Foster, *Prayer*, p. 7.
[9]*As Bill Sees It*, p. 321.
[10]As quoted in Armand Eisen, ed., *The Spiritual Life*, p. 74.
[11]As quoted in Eisen, *The Spiritual Life*, p. 258.
[12]As quoted in Eisen, *The Spiritual Life*, p. 46.
[13]As quoted in LaVonne Neff, *Breakfast with the Saints*, p.139.
[14]*New International Version Study Bible*, Deuteronomy 6:4–9.

7 • SOULMATES

[1]Nelly Kaufer and Carol Osmer-Newhouse, *A Woman's Guide to Spiritual Renewal*, p. 214.
[2]*The Living Bible*, Genesis 2:18.
[3]Avram Davis, *The Way of Flame*, p. 53.
[4]As quoted in Richard Carlson and Benjamin Shield, eds., *Handbook for the Soul*, p. 188.
[5]Dorothy Day, *The Long Loneliness*, p. 286.
[6]Sark, *Inspiration Sandwich*, p. 152.
[7]As quoted in Armand Eisen, ed., *The Spiritual Life*, p. 122.
[8]As quoted in David C. Gross and Esther R. Gross, compilers, *Jewish Wisdom*, p. 70.
[9]*The Living Bible*, Ecclesiasties 4:8–12.
[10]Paul Hinnebusch, O.P., *Friendship in the Lord*, p. 116.

8 • Soul Workout

[1]Thomas Merton, *Thoughts in Solitude*, p. 33.
[2]As quoted in Phil Cousineau, ed., *Soul, An Archaeology*, p. 101.
[3]Macrina Wiederkehr, O.S.B., *A Tree Full of Angels*, p. 90.
[4]As quoted in Richard J. Foster and James Bryan Smith, *Devotional Classics*, pp. 94–95.
[5]Ibid, p. 49.
[6]Thomas à Kempis, *The Imitation of Christ.*
[7]Edward Hays, *Prayers for a Planetary Pilgrim*, p. 250.
[8]St. John of the Cross. *Dark Night of the Soul.*
[9]Richard J. Foster, *Celebration of Disciplines*, p. 1.
[10]Slightly revised by the author.
[11]M. Basil Pennington, O.C.S.O., *A Place Apart*, p. 69–70.
[12]As quoted in David C. Gross and Esther R. Gross, compilers, *Jewish Wisdom*, p. 26.
[13]As quoted in Rabbi Hayim Halevy Donin, *To Be a Jew*, p. 245.

9 • Lightening Your Soul

[1]Karen Casey, *A Woman's Spirit*, January 16.
[2]Henri J. M. Nouwen, *Lifesigns*, pp. 102–3.
[3]Leslie Weatherhead as quoted in Elton Trueblood, *The Humor of Christ*, p. 25.

[4]Luci Swindoll, *After You've Dressed for Success*, p. 29.
[5]*The New International Version Holy Bible*, Ecclesiasties 3:1–8.
[6]*New American Standard Bible*, Psalm 30:5b.
[7]Luci Swindoll, *You Bring the Confetti*, p. 13.
[8]*The New International Version Holy Bible*, Philippians 4:8.
[9]Gerald May, "A Wink Out of Nowhere," *Shalem News*.
[10]Robert Fulghum, "Pay Attention," *Handbook for the Soul*, p. 14.
[11]As quoted in Casey, *A Woman's Spirit*, August 13.
[12]*The New International Version Holy Bible*, Proverbs 15:15.
[13]Richard J. Foster, *Celebration of Discipline*, p. 165.
[14]John Bailey, *Intent on Laughter*, p. 39.
[15]Patty Wooten, R.N., *Compassionate Laughter*, p. xiv.
[16]Raymond A. Moody, Jr., M.D., *Laugh After Laugh*, p. 13.
[17]*The New International Version Holy Bible*, Proverbs 15:13a.
[18]*The New International Version Holy Bible*, Proverbs 15:30a.
[19]Etty Hillesum, *An Interrupted Life*, New York: Holt, 1996.

[1]Paul Hinnebusch, O.P., *Friendship in the Lord*, p. 33.

[2]As quoted in Phil Cousineau, ed., *Soul, An Archaeology*, p. 142.

[3]Avram Davis, *The Way of Flame*, pp. 148–49.

[4]As quoted in Cousineau, *Soul, An Archaeology*, p. 140.

[5]*The New International Version Holy Bible*, Luke 6:27.

[6]Dan B. Allender, *The Wounded Heart*, pp. 221, 222, 223.

[7]As quoted in Armand Eisen, ed., *The Spiritual Life*, p. 289.

[8]As quoted in John K. Terres, *Things Precious and Wild*, p. 240.

[9]Frederick Buechner, *The Magnificent Defeat*, p. 65.

[10]Davis, *The Way of Flame*, p. 145.

[11]*The New International Version Holy Bible*, 1 John 2:9.

[12]C. S. Lewis, *The Four Loves*, p. 169.

[13]Eugene H. Peterson, *The Message*, 1 Corinthians 13:1–3.

[14]As quoted in Mary Ellen Ashcroft and Holly Bridges Elliott, *Bearing Our Sorrows*, p. 56.

[15]As quoted in Richard Carlson and Benjamin Shield, eds., *Handbook for the Soul*, p. 54.

[16] *The Joy of Words*, p. 35.

Afterword

[1] Frederick Buechner, *The Magnificent Defeat*, p. 91.

•BIBLIOGRAPHY•

Alcoholics Anonymous. Third Edition. New York: Alcoholics Anonymous World Services, Inc., 1976.

Allender, Dan B. *The Wounded Heart.* Colorado Springs, Colo.: NavPress, 1990.

Ashcroft, Mary Ellen & Elliott, Holly Bridges. *Bearing Our Sorrows.* San Francisco: HarperCollins, 1993.

As Bill Sees It. New York: Alcoholics Anonymous World Services, Inc., 1967.

Bailey, John. *Intent on Laughter.* New York: Quadrangle/The New York Times Book Co., 1976.

Bonny, Helen L. and Louis M. Savary. *Music & Your Mind: Listening with a New Consciousness.* Barrytown, N.Y.: Station Hill Press, 1973.

Buechner, Frederick. *The Magnificent Defeat.* New York: Harper & Row, 1966.

Carlson, Richard and Benjamin Shield, eds. *Handbook for the Soul.* New York: Little, Brown, 1995.

Casey, Karen. *A Woman's Spirit.* New York: HarperCollins, 1994.

Chambers, Oswald. *If You Will Ask.* Grand Rapids, Mich.: Discovery House, 1958.

Couchman, Judith. *Shaping a Woman's Soul.*

Grand Rapids, Mich.: Zondervan, 1996.
Cousineau, Phil, ed. *Soul, An Archaeology: Readings from Socrates to Ray Charles.* New York: HarperCollins, 1994.
Davis, Avram. *The Way of Flame: A Guide to the Forgotten Mystical Tradition of Jewish Meditation.* New York: HarperCollins, 1996.
Day, Dorothy. *The Long Loneliness.* San Francisco: Harper & Row, 1952.
Dillard, Annie. *The Writing Life.* New York: Harper & Row, 1989.
Durback, Robert, editor. *Seeds of Hope: Thoughts to Nourish a New Spirituality.* New York: Bantam, 1989.
Eisen, Armand, ed. *On Being Christian.* Kansas City, Mo.: Andrews and McMeel, 1995.
———. *The Spiritual Life: A Book of Reflections.* Kansas City, Mo.: Andrews and McMeel, 1995.
Foster, Richard J. *Celebration of Discipline: The Path to Spiritual Growth.* San Francisco: Harper & Row, 1978.
———. *Devotional Classics.* San Francisco: HarperCollins, 1990, 1991, 1993.
———. *Prayer: Finding the Heart's True Home.* New York: HarperCollins, 1992.
Gross, David C., and Esther R. Gross, compilers. *Jewish Wisdom.* New York: Fawcett Crest, 1992.

Hays, Edward. *Prayers for a Planetary Pilgrim.* 1988.

Hillesum, Etty. *Interrupted Life.* New York: Holt, 1996.

Hinnebusch, Paul, O.P. *Friendship in the Lord.* Notre Dame, Ind.: Ave Maria Press, 1974.

The Holy Bible, King James Version.

The Joy of Words. Chicago: J. G. Ferguson, 1960.

Kaufer, Nelly and Carol Osmer-Newhouse. *A Woman's Guide to Spiritual Renewal.* New York: HarperCollins, 1994.

Lewis, C. S. *The Four Loves.* New York: Harcourt Brace Jovanovich, 1960.

The Living Bible. Wheaton, Ill.: Tyndale House, 1971.

May, Gerald. "A Wink Out of Nowhere," *Shalem News*, Vol. 20, No. 2.

Merritt, Stephanie. *Mind, Music and Imagery: Unlocking Your Creative Potential.* New York: Penguin, 1990.

Merton, Thomas. *Thoughts in Solitude.* New York: Farrar, Straus and Giroux, 1956.

Moody, Raymond A., Jr., M.D. *Laugh After Laugh: The Healing Power of Humor.* Jacksonville, Fla.: Headwaters Press, 1978.

Neff, LaVonne. *Breakfast with the Saints.* Ann Arbor, Mich.: Servant Publications, 1966.

New American Standard Bible. La Habra, Cal.: The Lockman Foundation, 1960.

The New International Version Holy Bible. Colorado Springs, Colo. International Bible Society, 1984.

Nouwen, Henri J. M. *Lifesigns: Intimacy, Fecundity, and Ecstasy in Christian Perspective.* New York: Doubleday, 1986.

———. *Seeds of Hope: Thoughts to Nourish a New Spirituality.* Edited by Robert Durback. New York: Image Books, 1997.

Pennington, M. Basil, O.C.S.O., *A Place Apart: Monastic Prayer and Practice for Everyone.* Garden City, N.Y.: Doubleday, 1983.

Peterson, Eugene H. *The Message.* Colorado Springs, Colo. NavPress, 1994.

Pippert, Rebecca Manley. *Hope Has Its Reasons: From the Search for Self to the Surprise of Faith.* San Francisco: Harper & Row, 1989.

Post, Gregory and Charles Turner. *The Feast.* San Francisco: HarperCollins, 1992.

St. John of the Cross. *Dark Night of the Soul.* New York: Doubleday Image, 1990.

Sark. *Inspiration Sandwich: Stories to Inspire Our Creative Freedom.* Berkeley, Cal.: Celestial Arts, 1992.

Shaw, Lucy. *Water My Soul.* Grand Rapids,

Mich.: Zondervan, 1997.
Stone, Irving. *Depths of Glory: A Biographical Novel of Camille Pissarro.* New York: Doubleday, 1985.
Swindoll, Luci. *After You've Dressed for Success.* Dallas, Tex.: Word, Inc., 1987.
———. *You Bring the Confetti.* Dallas, Tex.: Word, Inc., 1986.
Tada, Joni Eareckson, Grand Rapids, Mich.: Zondervan, 1995.
Terres, John K. *Things Precious and Wild: A Book of Nature Quotations.* Golden, Colo.: Fulcrum, 1991.
Thomas à Kempis. *The Imitation of Christ*, trans. Harold C. Gardiner, S.J. New York: Doubleday, 1990.
Trueblood, Elton. *The Humor of Christ: A Significant But Often Unrecognized Aspect of Christ's Teaching.* New York: Harper & Row, 1964.
Tutu, Desmond. *An African Prayer Book.* New York: Doubleday, 1995.
Wiederkehr, Macrina, O.S.B., *A Tree Full of Angels: Seeing the Holy in the Ordinary.* San Francisco: Harper & Row, 1988.
Wooten, Patty, R.N. *Compassionate Laughter: Jest for Your Health.* Salt Lake City, Utah: Commune-A-Key, 1996.

•ABOUT THE AUTHORS•

TRACI MULLINS is president of Eclipse Editorial Services, which provides writing, editing, and concept development to a variety of corporate, nonprofit, and individual clients. For many years she was senior editor at Piñon Press and acquisitions editor at NavPress in Colorado Springs. She is the editor of more than eighty books and the author of *Breakfast with the Angels*.

ANN SPANGLER is the author of the best-selling *An Angel a Day*. Her recent books include *A Miracle a Day* and *Dreams*. Founding editor of Vine Books, she has served as vice president and editorial director at Servant Publications as well as senior acquisitions editor at Zondervan Publishing House.

DECATUR PUBLIC LIBRARY
3 1202 00538 1897